TALES FROM THE

DENVER BRONCOS
SIDELINE

TALES FROM THE
DENVER BRONCOS
SIDELINE

A COLLECTION OF THE GREATEST
BRONCOS STORIES EVER TOLD

ANDREW MASON

SPORTS
PUBLISHING

Sports Publishing books may be purchased in bulk at special discounts for sales promotion, corporate gifts, fund-raising, or educational purposes. Special editions can also be created to specifications. For details, contact the Special Sales Department, Sports Publishing, 307 West 36th Street, 11th Floor, New York, NY 10018 or sportspubbooks@skyhorsepublishing.com.

Sports Publishing® is a registered trademark of Skyhorse Publishing, Inc.®, a Delaware corporation.

Visit our website at www.sportspubbooks.com.

10 9 8 7 6 5 4 3 2 1

Library of Congress Cataloging-in-Publication Data is available on file.

Cover series design by Tom Lau
Cover photo credit: AP Photo

Print ISBN: 978-1-68358-134-5
Ebook ISBN: 978-1-68358-151-2

Printed in the United States of America

TO

My parents, who took me to NFL games at RFK Stadium and
Tampa Stadium and taught me to never leave early;

My wife, who tolerates my work and personal obsessions, all of
which have to do with sports;

My daughter, who can count on her dad reading this at bedtime
when she's older;

… And Broncos fans everywhere.

CONTENTS

From 18 to 18

March 19, 2012, was a gorgeous early spring day in the southern suburbs of Denver, and the Broncos were about to announce the signing of the National Football League's most coveted free agent since eventual Hall of Famer Reggie White. National media descended upon team headquarters to show Peyton Manning holding up a Broncos jersey, the symbol of a new era for both the team and the quarterback.

But there was just one problem. The Broncos weren't sure if No. 18 would be available.

No press conference for a signing of Manning's magnitude would be complete without the prize catch holding up the jersey with his name and number on it. That image would define the day—and the entire Broncos off-season—and would be splashed across sports pages and websites throughout North America and beyond.

But the Broncos could not send Manning up to the lectern in the team meeting room holding up a jersey number that he would never wear. He would be flanked by longtime owner Pat Bowlen and franchise guiding light John Elway, with a phalanx of cameras staring them down. The moment had to be just right: the speeches, the answers to questions, and the jersey that Manning would hold to show the world that that his Indianapolis Colts days were over for good and a nearly unprecedented next chapter was about to begin.

The No. 18 that Manning made famous in Indiana was retired for the Broncos' first quarterback, Frank Tripucka. He had last played forty-nine years ago in the rambunctious early days of the American Football League, and no one was sure whether it would be un-retired to give Manning the only number he had worn as a professional.

"I was fully prepared to wear No. 16, believe it or not, and go back to my college number," Manning would recall nearly two years later.

But Manning had worn No. 18 to carry on the football life of his elder brother. Cooper Manning had worn No. 18 in honor of their father, Archie; he donned it at the University of Mississippi and became so identified with it that to this day, speed limits on the Oxford, Mississippi, campus are 18 miles per hour.

There was only one person with whom Manning could speak: Tripucka. A week earlier, the old quarterback had given his blessing to bring the number out of retirement. But Manning, a keen student of the sport's history, would not don it without personal approval from the original Broncos' quarterback and his wife.

"Actually, they were not asking me, they were telling me that they really wanted me to wear No. 18," Manning said. "That would honor Frank."

"I let him know I would be honored," Tripucka said. "I have admired Peyton for a long time. He is one of the all-time greats, and having him wear the same jersey that I did, brings me a lot of joy."

The joy has extended to Broncos fans near and far. Manning's arrival heralded the Broncos' return to Super Bowl contention, spurring one of the best two-season runs in club history. He broke armfuls of franchise records. He reestablished Denver dominance in the same number that first established legitimacy for a flagging franchise in the American Football League a half-century earlier.

Manning fulfilled his promise, culminating with a 24-10 victory in Super Bowl 50, a game that would be Manning's last in an NFL uniform. It was his second Super Bowl with the Broncos, and by taking the team to their seventh and eighth Super Bowls in a three season span, the new No. 18 had returned the franchise to its place as one of the sport's elite and reminded younger generations of fans what made this number special in Broncos' history, now and forever. Unfortunately, Tripucka passed away in September, 2013, not having had the chance to see his old number appear on the sport's biggest stage.

Tripucka and Manning's shared number is the connective tissue between the Broncos' homely beginnings and their modern place among the game's elite. In between are the stories that define a club, a culture, and a profound connection between town and team.

CHAPTER ONE

The 1960s

IN THE BEGINNING ...

For those who are alternative history theorists, the formation of the Broncos and the American Football League at large represents one of those moments that if it had broken a bit differently, would have eventually created a 21st-century reality unrecognizable from the one that we know today.

That's because the Broncos' existence is at least partially due to the failure of a planned third baseball major league.

It was 1959, and for a city to be "major league" still meant only one thing: having a major league baseball franchise. Pro football was only beginning its rise; the teams of the National Football League still negotiated their own television contracts, creating a patchwork of rights fees and broadcast maps that remained a mishmash. The National Basketball Association still had a team in Syracuse, New York and was just two years removed from having a franchise in Fort Wayne, Indiana. The National Hockey League was still eight years away from expanding beyond its "Original Six."

Enter the Continental League, which proclaimed its existence on July 27, 1959. At its initial announcement, the circuit had five markets: Denver, New York City, Minneapolis-St. Paul, Houston, and Toronto. Denver and Houston were virgin territory for all professional sports when this announcement was made.

But the driving force behind the upstart start-up wasn't these overlooked markets throughout the continent, but the efforts of William A. Shea, Esq. to bring a major-league team to New York City. Shea—eventually, as in Shea Stadium—sought to replace the New York Giants and Brooklyn Dodgers, clubs that departed for San Francisco and Los Angeles following the 1957 season. But Shea couldn't start a new league without other cities, and the initial success of other 1950s relocations—in particular the Braves' shift from being poor second relations in Boston to breaking attendance records of the day in Milwaukee—revealed the growing appetite for big-league sports beyond the Northeast and Midwest clusters of cities that had dominated pro sports for decades.

Major League Baseball, a bit alarmed by the new league and the threat of losing its federal antitrust exemption, reacted swiftly. By 1962, MLB had expanded to Houston (the Colt 45's, later to be rechristened the Astros); had moved the Washington Senators to Bloomington, Minnesota, to become the Minnesota Twins; and had given Shea the National League team he really wanted, with the Mets beginning play at the Polo Grounds that the NL Giants abandoned. A second Los Angeles-area franchise was added with the Angels. Denver and Toronto would be left out in the MLB cold until 1977 and 1993, respectively.

But back in 1959, the quick death of the Continental League left Denver with little else on which it could hang its sports hat.

At that time, the biggest game in Denver was the University of Denver Pioneers college hockey team, which had won its first national championship the previous year and would become a dynasty, winning four titles in the 1960s. The latest iteration of the Denver Bears minorleague baseball team had built a following in the AAA American Association after moving from Kansas City, Missouri, in 1955. Bob Howsam ran those Bears, who played at Bears Stadium, a long fly ball west of downtown Denver. He helped spearhead an 8,000-seat expansion of the venue, presumably for a Continental League team. But with no baseball, he—and Denver—needed a reason to justify a bigger Bears Stadium.

That reason became the American Football League. In the same summer that Denver was connected to the Continental League, the city and Howsam were on much firmer footing as part of the AFL's "Foolish Club," the group of eight original owners who grew impatient with the NFL's deliberate attempts at its own expansion and wanted their piece of a pro football pie that was only beginning to grow.

"I wanted a football team here for the fans, because I thought we had great fans," Howsam later recalled of Denver's market worthiness for pro football. "I needed 35,000 seats to first, enter baseball, and second, we thought we could draw that many for football in time."

The AFL was already coming together when league founder—and team owner—Lamar Hunt came to Denver to meet with Howsam in the lobby of Denver's famed Brown Palace Hotel. In August 1959, the league's founding owners met in Chicago to officially bring the AFL into existence.

"They said, 'This is not going to work,'" Howsam's son, Robert Jr., said a half-century later. "Yeah, if you win a world championship, we'll give you some support. A Super Bowl wasn't even created yet. But he just said 'Hey, you've got to start somewhere.'"

Eventually, it did work—but not without some strain and not under Howsam's watch. He would sell the team after its first season to a local group led by local businessmen Gerald and Allan Phipps.

It wasn't until early 1960 that the new franchise had its name, reviving a minor-league baseball name from nearly four decades earlier. By then, it already had the rights to thirty-four players selected in the league's first draft—a dispersal of talent held before the Broncos even had initial general manager Dean Griffing in place.

WORKING UNDER A BUDGET

Griffing's plate quickly filled. But unlike the AFL's first titans, the Houston Oilers, he didn't have wealthy ownership to back him. The Oilers had the largesse of one-time wildcatter Bud Adams to back them up, and had used that to make the league's first splash. They signed 1959 Heisman Trophy winner Billy Cannon to a three-year, $110,000 contract—$60,000 more than the offer from the NFL's Los Angeles Rams. That made Cannon the first six-figure pro football player.

The Oilers promptly won the fledgling league's first two championships. Lamar Hunt's Dallas Texans and Ralph Wilson's Buffalo Bills also flourished in the league's early days as Hunt and Wilson were backed by personal and family fortunes that insured them against early losses.

On the other hand, the Broncos were run on a shoestring. Their budget was to be determined entirely by what they could take in. Their first headquarters building was a converted Quonset hut—"just like the Marines would have had," Howsam said, decades later. The players wore garish mustard-and-brown uniforms purchased from the Copper Bowl, a postseason all-star game held in Tucson, Arizona.

"They were the ugliest-looking things you ever wanted to see," quarterback Frank Tripucka recalled. "The sizes were very small. I had to cut the armpits in order to be able to put the jerseys on top of my shoulder pads, in order to raise my arm up."

The color scheme was bad enough, but the vertically striped socks—brown-and-yellow for home games; brown-and-white for road trips—capped the uniform, as it was, and made the Broncos a sartorial laughingstock.

"They made you look like a peg is what they did," said safety Austin "Goose" Gonsoulin. "You had these broad shoulders because of the pads and then you had these up-and-down striped socks. It was unique, put it that way."

But Griffing's background in the Canadian Football League proved invaluable in trying to be competitive with an ironclad financial bottom line. He reached back into his CFL roots for the Broncos' first head coach, former Saskatchewan Roughriders sideline boss Frank Filchock. They called on another ex-Roughrider, Frank Tripucka, to be the Broncos' first starting quarterback after he appeared set to retire; he had closed out the 1959 season as the Roughriders' interim coach following a brief stint with the Ottawa Rough Riders. They brought in players left and right.

"There were 120 guys in camp that first year," safety Austin "Goose" Gonsoulin said decades later. "I pulled a hamstring at one point and thought that was it. Guys would get cut or traded on the road, so I'd always bring a full suitcase, just in case."

It was a ragtag team, even by the standards of the fledgling circuit. But by July 1960, the Broncos were gathering at training camp. Major-league professional sports had come to Denver. Although no one realized it at the time, the truth is that the city and the entire Front

Range would never be the same again; this cowtown on the high prairie was about to grow up.

Howsam, his brother Earl, and Griffing did not use budgetary constraints as an excuse; they did their best with what they had. Given that such an ethos is a rallying cry of some successful baseball franchises today, it is appropriate that eventually Howsam would become one of that sport's finest executives, building the famed "Big Red Machine" as the Cincinnati Reds' general manager in the 1970s.

"Those owners were behind the team, even though we didn't have as much money as a lot of the other organizations had," said original Bronco Gene Mingo forty-nine years later. "But they did throw us what they could and they backed the team as best they could."

First Night

Nickerson Field on the Boston University campus has one of the more unusual histories in American sport. It sat on the same spot as Braves Field, where Boston's National League team played for thirty-eight seasons before moving to Milwaukee in 1953. It once had dimensions of 400 feet down the foul lines and 500 to straightaway center field. It was Babe Ruth's last home field; he played an unhappy twenty-eight games for the Braves before retiring in a huff following a tiff with owner Emil Fuchs. It has been at least a part-time home to teams from an alphabet soup of leagues: the USFL (Boston Breakers), the NASL (New England Tea Men), the MLL (Boston Cannons), and the WUSA (another iteration of Boston Breakers). No professional team ever played more than three seasons at Nickerson Field following its post-baseball renovation, not even the Boston Patriots.

But that's where they—and the Broncos—began their histories, and that of the American Football League.

The game on Friday night, September 9, 1960, was not televised. Prime-time football was a notion barely conceived, especially for a league that had barely begun to crawl. And the lights at Nickerson Field weren't bright enough for a viable nighttime broadcast, anyway.

But the Broncos lit up the night with big plays: quarterback Frank Tripucka's 59-yard pass to Al Carmichael for the first touchdown in AFL history, and then kicker/runner/receiver/returner Gene Mingo's 76-yard jaunt through the Patriots' punt-coverage team for the touchdown that eventually provided the winning points in a 13-10 triumph.

"When I caught it, I took a couple of steps to the right, back to the left and then cutting back to the right, I can see the blocking developing," Mingo would remember decades later. "As I ran down the sideline, somebody was reaching for me and another guy took him out. As I was going down the sidelines, coaches, players and everybody were waving for me to go on. I just kept running—running scared or whatever—but I made it into the end zone. I don't know if I ever ran that fast."

The only problem? The multi-talented Mingo was needed for the point-after-touchdown.

"I made it into the end zone and I was out of breath, tired and rubbery-legged. It was time for me to kick the extra point," he said. "I kicked this big divot; my leg was so dead."

But his lively legs on the punt return got the Broncos off to a promising start.

What Do You Do For an Encore?

The next day, one newspaper, the *Reading* (Pennsylvania) *Eagle*, curiously headlined the Broncos' win as an "upset," having bought into the bizarre notion that preseason results mattered—as was custom back in the day. The Broncos had lost their five preseason games by a combined 200-53 margin, including 43-6 to the Patriots in the opener of the warm-up slate. It didn't help that the Broncos had not played one preseason game within 750 miles of Denver; the closest they came was a trip to Little Rock, Arkansas, where they were slaughtered by the Dallas Texans 48-0 in front of a quiet, roughly estimated crowd of 5,500.

Two more road trips followed the win at Boston. During most of their time away from Denver, the Broncos lived at a hotel in Plainfield, New Jersey, looking to minimize their cross-country trips.

The Broncos wouldn't finally play in front of the home fans until October 2, four weeks into the regular season. In front of a crowd of 18,372 that filled barely half of the expanded Bears Stadium, Denver defeated the Oakland Raiders 31-14 to move to 3-1. It was the first of five consecutive home games. As the weeks progressed, attendance began to lag, along with the team's performance. A 31-24 win over Boston in the third game of the homestand was the last win of the season, and the Broncos fell from 4-2 midway through October to 4-9-1 by the end of the season.

"We were not that good a football team," Tripucka would recall four decades later. "Whenever we would pull one out, it was always exciting."

The Unexpected Quarterback

By the time Frank Tripucka joined the Broncos' first training camp at the Colorado School of Mines in Golden, he was already a former professional head coach.

Even before Tripucka was aware that vertically striped socks existed, he had the unique distinction of being the only professional coach to lead his team to a win that had already gone into the books as a forfeit loss—all because he'd inserted himself into the lineup at quarterback because of injuries. He did this for two games with the Canadian Football League's Saskatchewan Roughriders in 1959: one a 20-19 defeat, the other a stunning 37-30 win over the Winnipeg Blue Bombers. Thus, even before he threw a pass in Denver, Tripucka had a win as a coach over a future Hall of Fame coach: Bud Grant, who would eventually coach the Vikings from 1967 to 1983 and in 1985.

Amazingly, this might not have been the most unusual circumstance to befall Tripucka as a pro. In 1952, he was in his fourth season as an NFL quarterback, having hopscotched from the Detroit Lions to the Chicago Cardinals and then on to the NFL's version of the Dallas Texans—the latter of which lasted just a single, depressing season. The Texans would be the last NFL team to fold, and by the end of the season, they played their "home" games in Akron, Ohio, and Hershey, Pennsylvania. But before they went extinct, Tripucka led the hapless Texans to a 27-23 upset over the Chicago Bears, allowing them to avert going 0-for-their-history.

Everything the Broncos endured in their first years—a tight budget, living in a motel during an extended East Coast swing, an outmanned roster—was something that Tripucka had seen before. He was ideally suited to the role of being the Broncos' first quarterback, especially in a league that had former NFL backups like the New York Titans' Al Dorow and the Houston Oilers' George Blanda enjoying renaissances.

But when Frank Filchock summoned then thirty-two–year-old Tripucka to Denver in the summer of 1960, it was not to play, but to continue the coaching career in which he took his tentative steps in Saskatchewan.

"Frank Filchock was the head coach and he was trying to put a team together," Tripucka recalled in 2006. "I knew Frank from up in

Canada, up in the CFL. I had come home and Filchock called me up and said, 'How about you come up to our training camp and help out with our quarterbacks?' So I told him that I would be happy to. I wasn't doing a lot at the time so I went out there.

"Next thing you know they are playing a [preseason] game and we couldn't complete a pass. They had charged five bucks a head to get into the game. So Filchock says to me at halftime, 'You better get dressed and get in there. Give these people their five dollars worth.' So I went in and played the rest of the half and then I played the rest of the four seasons."

ONE-HANDED GENIUS

As much as Tripucka brought to the table on his own, his success in Denver would not have been possible without the presence of Lionel Taylor. A year after Tripucka notched the first 3,000-yard season in U.S. pro football history, Taylor became the first 100-catch receiver in the sport.

But unlike Tripucka, Taylor didn't come to the AFL looking to hang on for another few years. He had played the 1959 season for George Halas' Chicago Bears and regarded the upstart league as a road back to the senior circuit.

"I was in the NFL and I didn't think the AFL would make it, but I thought if I went over to the AFL and made a name for myself, I could come back to the NFL and make some money," Taylor recalled. "As it turned out, it was the greatest thing that ever happened to me because I never went back to the NFL."

For Tripucka, Taylor's arrival at practice three weeks into the 1960 season was heaven-sent.

"We were playing one of Frank Filchock's touch football games; instead of practicing, we were running pass patterns," he remembered.

"All of a sudden, Lionel makes a couple of one-handed grabs. Filchock sees this, and he stops practice. And all of a sudden we're running new pass patterns to see whether this guy is for real or whether he can only do this in a touch football game."

He was as real as it got. That week, he caught six passes for 125 yards and a touchdown in a 28-24 loss to the New York Titans.

"You put that ball anyplace near him, he was going to catch it, no question about it," Tripucka said.

A technically gifted receiver who didn't have elite speed but ran precise routes and caught everything in sight, Taylor spent twenty-five years after his career passing on his tips as a coach. His career was highlighted by head-coaching stops at Texas Southern University for five seasons and the London/England Monarchs of NFL Europe for three more.

THE MOST VERSATILE BRONCO

No player bleeds orange and blue—and mustard and brown, too— quite like Gene Mingo, the man responsible for scoring seven of the Broncos' 13 points in the franchise opener—and then 401 more over the Broncos' first five seasons.

And perhaps no Bronco came more out of the blue. He didn't play college football and while living in Akron, Ohio, wrote Filchock a letter asking for a tryout. His request was successful and he became the most versatile player in franchise history, displaying this from the outset by kicking the first extra point in Broncos and AFL history and posting the first touchdown via a return in league annals, a 76-yard dash that provided the game-winning points in the 13-10 win at Boston.

Mingo was just twenty-one when he made his professional debut, and over the next four seasons he kicked 120 extra points, 72 field goals and scored 12 touchdowns—three receiving, eight rushing, and one via his opening-night return.

Mingo would go on to kick for the Oakland Raiders, Miami Dolphins, Washington Redskins, and Pittsburgh Steelers. In Miami, he kicked the first extra point in Dolphins history, drilling the point after following Joe Auer's franchise-opening 95-yard kickoff return on September 2, 1966. Mingo would also notch the extra points following Terry Bradshaw's first professional touchdown run and pass in 1970.

By then, Mingo's accuracy wasn't what it was in Denver. But he still mined a ten-year career out of a single optimistic letter. Rarely has four cents—the cost of a stamp in 1960—reaped such a bountiful harvest.

THE HARDEST HITTER

"Probably the hardest-hitting back ever to come out of the Missouri Valley Conference" is the euphemistic description from the 1960 Broncos media guide of linebacker Hardy Brown.

Had Brown played in the 21st century, he might have racked up so many fines that he would have been playing to pay—that is, unless his suspensions had been so voluminous that they resulted in a perpetual on-field ban. Brown's existence was hard; he grew up in a Fort Worth, Texas, orphanage. Early on, he developed a habit of launching himself into players, often using his shoulder to lead into a player's chin. This was before face masks were mandatory, too.

Long before beginning his NFL career, Brown was a Marine paratrooper in the Pacific theater during the Second World War. He matriculated at the University of Tulsa before he broke into pro football in 1948 with the Brooklyn Dodgers of the All-America Football Conference—the league that gave the NFL the San Francisco 49ers, Cleveland Browns, and the first iteration of the Baltimore Colts.

Brown was accused of accentuating his hits by wearing metal under his shoulder pads.

"They thought maybe he was using a steel plate or something," Gordy Soltau, a teammate of Brown's for five seasons with the 49ers, told the *San Francisco Examiner* in 1993, "George Halas, the Bears coach, sent an official into our locker room right before one game. They made Hardy take off his shoulder pads, thinking he had some metal in there. But he didn't."

By the time Brown landed with the Broncos in 1960, face masks were mandated, and Brown hadn't played a professional football game in four years before the new team inserted him at middle linebacker. But he unleashed his shoulder just as he always had. Even though Brown played just one season for the Broncos, no list of the team's most feared hitters is complete without him.

In the end, the shoulder shots exacted a heavy price. He suffered from arthritis in that shoulder, which was only the beginning of his health problems; in 1991, he died suffering from Alzheimer's disease and emphysema.

Nearly forty-nine years after Brown's final shoulder shot, an NFL Network program on the game's hardest hitters of all time ranked him fifth. After all these years, the legend of Brown's ferocity remains secure.

CHANGE AT THE TOP

After the 1960 season, Bob Howsam sold the Broncos to a consortium called Rocky Mountain Empire Sports, whose primary financial and management thrust came from Cal Kunz and the Phipps brothers, Gerald and Allan. Together, the Phippses controlled 42 percent of the team, and given their local prominence, they were the most visible members of the consortium.

But team ownership wasn't the clearest path to a profitable venture. In the group's first year of stewardship, the Broncos lost $300,000. That didn't faze its members, but they learned they had to spend money to make money.

"We studied the history of the National Football League and the future of the AFL and felt the Broncos would eventually be our moneymakers," Phipps said at the time. "But we decided after that that it was going to take a lot more spending this year."

And a lot of alterations to the organization, too. But they would wait until after the season.

SECOND VERSE: SAME AS THE FIRST

After a 1-4 preseason in which the Broncos had so many injuries that they had to cancel an intra-squad scrimmage, they opened 1961 as they did 1960: with a stunning win on the road defeating the well-heeled Buffalo Bills 22-10.

But as was the case in 1960, they hung in contention for a while, and hit midseason at 3-4 following a pair of home wins over Oakland and the New York Titans. But just like 1960, the Broncos collapsed in the second half of the season, in which the Broncos went winless and lost by an average of 22.4 points per game.

Following that seven-game skid, the first head coach became the first head coach to be fired, when Filchock was dismissed. He departed with a 7-20-1 record.

The Broncos couldn't play hard-nosed, defensive football. Some of that was due to budget constraints, which led to a lack of talent. But Filchock's practice philosophy did not help.

"His big thing in practice was, 'Let's play a touch football game,'" Tripucka said, decades later. "And he'd play this game for two hours straight. And that's what he considered his practice sessions."

Filchock was quickly replaced by San Diego Chargers assistant Jack Faulkner, who had helped guide them to a 12-2 record and appearance in the AFL Championship Game.

At thirty-five, Faulkner became the AFL's youngest coach. He wasted little time in proclaiming, "There's lots new in '62." It became the slogan and the rallying cry.

SAYONARA, SOCKS

Faulkner's arrival was the first piece of evidence that the new ownership was serious about getting pro football right in Colorado. The second piece came when he quickly ditched the reviled colors and socks in favor of orange and blue and a more muted, traditional football look.

"We'll definitely get rid of those vertical-striped socks," said team president Cal Kunz at the time. "But it really wasn't the socks that bothered me last season [1961]. It was the guys wearing them."

Nevertheless, the uniforms had come to symbolize everything that was askew about the Broncos—and by extension, the still-fledgling league.

The pass-intensive offenses of the AFL provided an attractive product and its elite teams were starting to raise some eyebrows in the pro football establishment. But the AFL chain was only as strong as its weakest links. At the time, these were in Oakland, Denver, and New York, where broadcaster Harry Wismer tried to run his New York Titans on a small-town budget in the nation's largest media market. The Titans' paychecks often bounced. They had no scouting to speak of and in 1961, their entire draft preparation consisted of reading a copy of *Street & Smith's College Football Annual.*

By comparison, the Broncos were a well-oiled operation. Their defense leaked touchdowns and wins were scarce but Taylor was emerging as a legitimate AFL star having caught 100 passes in a 1961 season in which the Broncos went 3-11. The Phippses were prominent in Denver business, legal, and society circles, and their stewardship conferred a measure of local respect on an operation that many still regarded with curiosity and caution.

But the uniforms—oh, those uniforms. It would be four-and-a-half decades before they would be regarded with ironic fondness. In 1962, they had to go, and be dispatched in most dramatic fashion possible. So during the preseason, Faulkner organized a burning of the reviled footwear. Only a few socks survived, and one sits in a frame at Broncos headquarters to this day.

The Broncos looked like winners for the first time. And perhaps not coincidentally, they played like winners, stunning the AFL by sprinting to a 6-1 record.

SHAPING UP UNDER FAULKNER

Faulkner tightened the Broncos' ship. The "touch football" practices of the Filchock era vanished. Curfews were enforced. Players wore coats and ties on road trips and could not smoke in public. Football was on his mind nearly every moment of the day.

No one was more impressed than Tripucka.

"We always had the talent," he said early in the 1962 season. "But we never had organization. We used to make up plays in the huddle: 'OK, who wants to run out for a pass?' And on blocking assignments at the line of scrimmage I was up there pointing to the guys on the other team: 'Somebody better get him. Somebody better take him.'"

All that changed under Faulkner.

"Now here is an organizer," Tripucka said. "This team will go now."

By November, the Broncos were 7-2 and sprinting toward a berth in the AFL Championship Game, leading the Western Division. And even if they fell short, all they needed for their first winning season was one more win or tie. But a 33-29 loss at Boston knocked them off-kilter and the next week they were throttled by West rivals Dallas 24-3.

Still, no loss was more crushing than a 46-45 defeat to the New York Titans on Thanksgiving Day at Bears Stadium. Leading 45-32 with less than five minutes remaining, the Broncos collapsed, allowing a 65-yard touchdown march, then fumbling on their next play from scrimmage. The Titans scored three plays later to take a one-point lead that held up when Gene Mingo's desperation 52-yard field-goal attempt was short and wide.

In spite of the Broncos' late fade, Faulkner's work earned him AFL Coach of the Year honors. But the Broncos had allowed 30.8 points a game in the losing streak. It was a harbinger of what was to come the following season when the Broncos opened with what is still their worst home loss, a 59-7 throttling by the Kansas City Chiefs, in their first game with a new name after moving from Dallas in the off-season.

ONE MORE ENCORE, FRANKIE

Tripucka had more aborted notions of retirement than Brett Favre, and his threats of a retirement were an annual tradition in the Broncos' early years. However, every time, something brought him back: a chance to keep throwing to Taylor, a coaching change, new socks.

Football had a grasp on the former Notre Dame quarterback. But by the time he was thirty-five years old, he was pragmatic, and after tossing a 20-yard touchdown to Lionel Taylor to seal a 21-14 AFL All-Star Game win for the West team, he acknowledged that if he returned for a fourth Broncos season, it was about the cash.

"It would take a fantastic amount of money to get me back next year," he said in announcing his retirement after the game.

Lo and behold, by next summer, there was Tripucka, back under center, trying to get the Broncos over the hump for their first winning season after the .500 finish of the previous year. But he struggled in two starts and retired—apparently for good.

That ended Tripucka's time in Denver. But in Tripucka's grand tradition, it wasn't the curtain on his professional career; he un-retired once again to briefly return to Saskatchewan before finally hanging up his helmet for good.

With that, his whistle-stop football career ended. But his name wasn't done on the national stage.

Frank's son Kelly carried on the family name in professional sports. He followed in his father's footsteps by attending Notre Dame but played basketball and went on to a twelve-year career in the NBA. And like his father, Kelly was the first star of an expansion team, joining the Charlotte Hornets for their first season in 1988-89 and leading them in scoring.

But those Hornets eventually left; in taking the opposite path of the Broncos, they started with league-leading attendance that declined for myriad reasons. The Broncos stayed, and in gratitude to Tripucka's stabilizing presence in the early days, retired his number in 1984. Tripucka gave his blessing for it to be unretired for Peyton Manning, but as soon as the modern No. 18 hung up the helmet, the number went back into history again, shared by two quarterbacks divided by a half-century but bound by their leadership abilities and importance to the franchise.

Tripucka supported the Broncos until his death on September 12, 2013, in New Jersey, the home state to which he returned after his playing days. A day later, the Broncos arrived for their upcoming game against the New York Giants and Tripucka's sons and Manning met for a heartfelt time together. They shared memories and closed the circle that began when Frank Tripucka was pressed into service and began building the Broncos' foundation.

"LEND-LEASE LEE"

In soccer leagues around the globe, the notion of "lending" a player to another team for a stint is common for myriad reasons, although it is typically described as "loaning." Almost all of them involve playing time, although the concerns are different given the age and experience of the player being requested for a loan.

In American football, that doesn't happen—at least not in the last half-century. But in August 1964, the Broncos sent cash and All-AFL defensive tackle Bud McFadin, a draft pick, to the Houston Oilers for quarterback Jacky Lee.

There was a catch: by 1966, the Broncos had to give Lee back to Houston. Thus, Lee became known as "Lend-Lease Lee." It's not a moniker he liked then—or decades later, for that matter.

"Me being a little bullheaded, it didn't make sense to me," Lee would say after being returned to Houston in 1966. "The Oilers tried to make me see it realistically and optimistically, but at the beginning I was real bitter."

Even though Denver offered Lee a chance to start after being George Blanda's backup in Houston for four years, being shipped from the relatively well-heeled Oilers to the hardscrabble Broncos was like exchanging

Rodeo Drive for Tobacco Road. But the plan was for Lee to gain experience, then return to Houston—presumably to succeed Blanda.

It didn't do anything to help the perception of the Broncos. In what some pro football cognoscenti considered a minor league anyway, a deal like this gave the appearance that the Broncos were a farm team within it.

Faulkner was Lee's position coach at the University of Cincinnati, so he thought he knew what he was getting. But Lee never panned out as he hoped, throwing nearly twice as many interceptions (20) as touchdowns (11) in 1964. Faulkner was fired after Lee and the Broncos stumbled to an 0-4 opening, having won just two of twenty-three games after the 7-2 start in 1962. Lee started ten of the first eleven games in 1964, but fell out of favor under new coach Mac Speedie, and started just one game in the 4-10 season of 1965, with Mickey Slaughter and John McCormick starting the rest.

That ended Lee's loan. He quietly returned to Houston—experienced, but not necessarily pleased with how he got there.

"When I got the opportunity to play [in Denver] I began to recognize defenses," Lee said in 1966. "And I had very little coaching up there. It was just a bad situation. But as bad as the situation was, it did turn out for the best."

In every way, at least in terms of team accomplishments. Although he never established himself as a solid starter, Lee's road eventually wound to Kansas City where he won a Super Bowl ring as Len Dawson's backup for Super Bowl IV.

A TEAM IN TROUBLE

Failure on the field led to struggles at the gate. By 1964, attendance was cratering in Denver, even as its AFL rivals were on increasingly solid footing. Lamar Hunt's Dallas franchise, worn down by the competition from the NFL's Cowboys, moved to Kansas City and found an audience. The Chargers had been in San Diego for three years after an opening season in Los Angeles. The Raiders, a 9-33 joke their first three seasons, emerged after hiring Al Davis as head coach and general manager in 1963; they would remain a perennial contender for the next thirty years. Even woebegone New York was flourishing after ownership transferred from Wismer to television and recording-industry magnate Sonny Werblin. He knew glitz, glamour, and how to get his team noticed in Manhattan. All that came together in his 1965 signing of Joe Namath, and the Jets were at cruising altitude.

Meanwhile, the AFL's presence on national television exploded. A new five-year contract with NBC to begin in the 1965 season tripled revenues over what the league made from ABC in its first deal. The league and its teams were on the upswing. Its wide-open games continued to attract notice. Only one straggler remained: Denver, with attendance that had fallen from the league's third-highest average in 1962 (25,498) to dead last in 1964. The average crowd of 16,894 at Bears Stadium that season was 33.7 percent below 1962's pace. The Broncos' arrow pointed in the wrong direction. Some of the members of Rocky Mountain Empire Sports wanted a way out of the red ink. And cities without pro football longingly eyed a way in, and the predators prepared to pounce on the gasping Broncos as the prime candidates for relocation.

In previous decades, a pro football team folding was a legitimate possibility; as recently as 1952, the NFL version of the Dallas Texans folded after just one season in the market. But by 1965, pro football was muscling its way to the apex of the American sports pyramid and the demand for the Broncos was fierce. Interested markets included Cincinnati, New Orleans, Seattle, and even Philadelphia and Chicago, where owners lined up to for a chance to challenge their city's NFL operation.

But no threat was more serious than the one from Atlanta. Emboldened by the imminent relocation of the National League Braves from Milwaukee to play in shiny Atlanta Stadium for the 1966 season, the city wanted a professional football franchise as a complement to cement the New South's big-league status. An offer from Atlanta was made, worth a reported $6 million—an astronomical sum given that the original AFL franchise fee just six years earlier was $25,000.

With that sort of money being tossed about, other owners in the AFL seemed perfectly willing to open the stable and let the Broncos gallop south.

THE PHIPPSES SAVE THE DAY

As Gerald Phipps told *Sports Illustrated* at the time: "I had visits from two very fine men—Sonny Werblin of the New York Jets and Ralph Wilson of the Buffalo Bills. They tried to convince me the Broncos ought to get out of Denver for the good of the league. They considered Denver a detriment to the AFL, and at the time they were right."

The Broncos had sold just 8,002 season tickets for the 1964 season, in which they went 2-11-1 for a second consecutive year. To this day, these remain the two worst seasons in team history, and they came at the worst possible point: when the club was still fledgling and fragile. A stiff economic gust would be enough to knock down the entire operation, even with the increased television money from NBC set to transform every AFL club's bottom line.

But the Phippses declined Atlanta's offer on Valentine's Day, 1965. A day later, having taken out a seven-figure loan, Gerald Phipps turned to Cal Kunz and offered $1.5 million for the 52 percent of the franchise controlled by Kunz and the investors he represented. On February 16, the Broncos announced that the Phippses had 94 percent of the team and that it would stay in Denver.

Denver responded to the valentine with unbridled love of its own. Knowing what would be lost if the Broncos had left, a ticket drive set a goal of 20,000 season tickets. They moved fast.

Gerald Phipps felt the affection, but for him, the decision to increase his investment was as much practical as emotional. As he said at the time:

"Why do we want to keep the Broncos in Denver? I could sell out and make a potful of money. We're not kidding ourselves that this will ever be a gold mine here. But we're trying to attract industry to this community. Nothing would hurt us more than headlines around the country saying Denver had lost its football team. I would be cutting my own throat if I did something that would set back the community, and if we can sell 20,000 season tickets we can break even financially."

And the Broncos took a novel approach to reach that goal. Instead of turning to corporations, they focused on fans who became the heart and soul of the organization. This wouldn't be like Green Bay, where locals own shares of the Packers, but the fans felt invested. Local businessmen like construction magnate Nick Petry led the way. Denver-area banks got involved to help finance their season-ticket plans.

"I'd rather sell 1,000 individuals one ticket each than sell 1,000 tickets to one big company," Petry said in 1965. "A sidewalk and country-road alumni is what we want. When it is snowing or the team is not doing well, the individual fan who has bought his own ticket will be at the game."

The goal of 20,000 season tickets was hit by April, in a stampede to spend unseen since the Gold Rush days. The number would eventually climb above 23,000. The on-field performance was much the same for the short term, but attendance rocketed from dead last in the league in attendance to fourth, with a 31,398 average that nearly doubled the previous year's total.

But the job was not done. Bears Stadium, expanded just five years earlier, would not be sufficient for the future. The AFL's recent poaching of Joe Namath for the rechristened New York Jets was the warning shot that began pushing the AFL and NFL toward conciliation and a merger before both sides destroyed each other in a building bidding war featuring a fusillade of mammoth contracts to unproven college players.

"I know we're going to have to have a bigger stadium," Phipps acknowledged. "We can't really compete unless we have 50,000 seats. I think what we'll do is add on to the stadium we have."

That would be the Broncos' primary off-field task for the rest of the decade.

On the Field, More of the Same

Buoyed by the season-ticket drive, the Broncos upgraded their roster with a pair of AFL stars: fullback Cookie Gilchrist and halfback Abner Haynes, both acquired in the off-season. Quarterback was still a massive question mark; none of the three passers on hand was a potential answer. But the massive 251-pound Gilchrist was arguably the best big back in the game, having averaged 1,018.7 yards a season and 4.5 yards a carry the previous three seasons in Buffalo.

Meanwhile, Haynes was a few decades ahead of his time: a 190-pound running back who was at least as effective catching passes as taking handoffs. He averaged 39.8 receptions a year before coming to the Broncos and was coming off a year in which he racked up 1,259 yards from scrimmage. He was also one of the league's best kickoff returners.

"Between us, Cookie and me, we'll gain 2,000 yards this year," Haynes proclaimed in the preseason.

He hadn't counted on the hindrance of playing behind an offensive line that had been one of the AFL's worst since Tripucka's heyday. Although Gilchrist ran for 954 yards, his per-carry average dropped to 3.8 as good holes were hard to find. His 252 carries set what was then an AFL record. Haynes flourished as an All-AFL returner, but had the worst season of his career in yards from scrimmage. The duo combined for 1,490 yards from scrimmage—productive, but not what Haynes, Gilchrist, or the Broncos expected.

How the "Cookie" Crumbles

Carlton Chester "Cookie" Gilchrist arrived—late—to his first Broncos training camp in 1965 in a gold Cadillac that had its own telephone, and, supposedly, its own television.

He was ahead of his time in another way beyond in-car technology: his awareness of contractual issues and finances. Years later, in an interview with the *Montreal Gazette*, he whipped out a pen and paper and wrote down exactly how much he earned for each of his CFL and AFL seasons. He wanted to be paid what he perceived as a fair amount for his services, and took an active interest in off-field business ventures to supplement his income.

Gilchrist also took stands for larger issues. Most nobly, he led a player boycott of the 1964 AFL All-Star Game which was scheduled for still-racially segregated New Orleans. The action worked and the game was moved to Houston.

But Gilchrist's independent streak manifested itself in other ways that rubbed coaches and management the wrong way. The reason he was available to the Broncos via trade (for fullback Billy Joe) was because Buffalo Bills head coach Lou Saban had tired of Gilchrist's act, which at one point included walking off the field during a 1964 game, leading to a suspension. He was later reinstated and led the Bills to that year's AFL title, running for 122 yards in a 20-7 championship-game win.

Gilchrist brought one of the oddest contract demands ever created, one that stemmed from his prior experience. In addition to playing fullback, he was a kicker and a defensive lineman during his earlier days in the Canadian Football League. He believed extra tasks merited extra pay.

"I did two guys' work and was getting half of what I deserved," he said after his career was over.

So when he arrived in Denver, he expressed willingness to play a versatile role, but with a catch: he suggested to Broncos management that they draw up three different contracts, one for each phase of the game if they wanted him to play ironman football.

"Stick to fullback," came the reply.

The pattern of contentious dialogue between Gilchrist and management continued. At one point the Broncos filed a breach-of-contract lawsuit against him. He didn't report on time for training camp in 1965 or 1966 and the exasperated Broncos traded him to the expansion Miami Dolphins.

But that wasn't the end for Gilchrist in Denver. His old coach, Saban, brought him back in 1967 at the age of thirty-two after accepting the Broncos' coaching job. However, Gilchrist injured his knee in the first regular-season game and never played again.

To this day, Gilchrist isn't given the credit he deserves for being one of the best big backs—and unusual characters—the game has ever known.

Beating an NFL Team: More than "Just Preseason"

The Green Bay Packers' 35-10 win over the Kansas City Chiefs in the first Super Bowl established NFL dominance—for the moment. But with the AFL-NFL merger still three years away and no inter-league play in the regular season, the only chances most AFL clubs would have to prove their worth was in a series of preseason games against the older league.

Denver's turn came on August 5, 1967, when the Broncos hosted the Detroit Lions. Their snarling defensive tackle, Alex Karras, didn't think much of the notion of playing an AFL team and was more certain of victory. The future actor and broadcaster was never one to restrain his sentiments and told Detroit media, "If we lose to the Denver Broncos, I'll walk back to Detroit."

Not only did the Broncos win, but also they became the first AFL side to knock off an NFL team. Given that the Broncos were the AFL's perennial cellar dwellers, it struck a crushing blow to the notion that the only team capable of competing against even a weak NFL side was the defending champions from Kansas City.

"Denver wanted it more than we did," said a dejected Joe Schmidt, the Lions coach who was in his first game on the job.

The Broncos played with aggression that would seem foreign to today's preseason play. Punter Bob Scarpitto gained 28 yards on a fake punt to set up a Cookie Gilchrist touchdown run. The next week, the Broncos had a perfect encore, defeating the NFL's Minnesota Vikings 14-3 and proving the win over the Lions was not a fluke.

Oh, and Karras? He flew back to Detroit with his teammates after having been ejected for kicking Gilchrist. The closest he came to walking around Denver was stalking an Old West town as Mongo in Mel Brooks' *Blazing Saddles* seven years later.

AN EMPTY GLASS FROM THE DRAFT

The American Football League draft was an exercise in high hopes but futile results for the Broncos in their first years. It wasn't that they drafted lousy players; to the contrary, the Broncos' first-round picks in the AFL Draft included defensive tackle Merlin Olsen, offensive lineman Bob "Boomer" Brown, and, in 1965, linebacker Dick Butkus. All would eventually be Pro Football Hall of Famers—but did so for teams in the "other" league with which they signed.

The 1960 drafts to stock the entirely expansion league were only announced in alphabetical order, so there were no picks recorded by round. Roger LeClerc, a kicker and offensive lineman from Trinity (Connecticut) College, was the first Broncos pick of that expansion draft and was never signed—a harbinger of what was to come.

Nevertheless, from the next draft onward, the new league, rambunctious with hope and desperate for attention, was only too happy to trumpet first-round status on the college stars its teams would court.

But the Broncos were the perpetual spinsters of the bunch. From the AFL's college drafts of 1961–66, only one Broncos first-round pick ever played with the team: New Mexico State halfback Bob Gaiters, who was the No. 1 overall pick in the 1961 draft. To get a jump on the NFL, that draft was actually held on December 5 and 6, 1960.

Gaiters eventually played six games with Denver in 1963—but only after he had washed out of the NFL because of a nasty case of "fumblitis." He coughed up eleven fumbles in his rookie season with the New York Giants, who selected him the second round of the 1961 NFL Draft—which, like the AFL's, was held in 1960, although it did not begin until December 27.

The Broncos' failures at reeling in their first rounders was typical of the AFL in those days; signings like the Houston Oilers' procurement of Heisman Trophy winner Billy Cannon for the 1960 season were rare. That's why the 1965 signing of Joe Namath by the New York Jets was arguably the touchstone moment of the nascent league. It required a perfect storm of massive media market, deep-pocketed ownership, and the presence of a coach, Weeb Ewbank, who oozed credibility from the NFL championships he won with the Baltimore Colts and quarterback Johnny Unitas in 1958 and 1959.

The Namath signing was also the beginning of the end for the AFL Draft. The next year's draft saw offensive tackle Jerry Shay spurn the Broncos for the Minnesota Vikings, but by then the wheels were in motion for a merger of the two leagues. Owners understandably chafed at the notion of bidding wars for untested rookies, and on June 8, 1966, the NFL and AFL announced their merger, which would be phased in over the next four years.

RAISING MILE HIGH

One consequence of the merger was a mandate that all stadia have a capacity of at least 50,000. That wasn't a problem for most of the AFL; of the eight other clubs in the league by 1966 after the expansion to Miami, three were already in new venues or had them under construction and two others already played in stadia that met the qualification.

But at that time, Bears Stadium was just six years removed from its expansion to accommodate the Broncos, and even after the ticket drive of 1965, the Broncos still played slightly below capacity. It was into this environment that a bond issue was placed before voters in four metropolitan Denver counties—Adams, Arapahoe, Denver and Jefferson—to build a new, multipurpose stadium at a taxpayer cost of $20 million.

Colorado voters were reluctant to approve such measures in those days. Five and a half years later, the state's voters resoundingly rejected using public funds to finance the hosting of the 1976 Winter Olympic Games, citing myriad reasons from taxes to environmental impact. The state had been selected as host two years earlier, with a plan that called for the Games to be based in Denver but for some events to be held all the way to Steamboat Springs, 125 miles northwest. Thus, Denver became the first—and only—host to turn down the Olympics, which were moved to Innsbruck, Austria.

So in retrospect, it was no surprise that on March 7, 1967, Denver-area voters rejected the new-stadium measure by a nearly two-to-one margin, although it stunned the Broncos and their most devoted supporters. By the end of the month, it was 1965 all over again, as Gerald Phipps announced he had two offers for the club: an $8 million bid from Phoenix and a "tentative" $10 million offer from a group in Birmingham, Alabama.

Phipps understood that football was a business, but his roots in the community reminded him that the Broncos were a public trust as well. So he hesitated on the bids. That bought time for a consortium of local supporters calling themselves the DOERS—Denver Organization to Erect the Right Kind of Stadium—to begin raising money. Their plan was to raise $1.8 million, buy Bears Stadium from the Phipps Brothers, and then gift the stadium to the city and county of Denver. After that, the city would issue bonds to pay for a 16,000-seat expansion that built two upper levels on the west stands and pushed the capacity to the magic 50,000 number.

Significant, six-figure chunks of revenue came from locally-based, large businesses like Mountain Bell, Gates Rubber Co., and Coors. Fans pitched in with donations. By the summer, the money was raised and expansion plans could proceed. The Phipps brothers kept the team. And Broncos fans would again step forward to buy tickets; by 1969, the average attendance rose to 46,579—nearly three times what it was in 1964, before the first drive to save the team.

With the city and county now in control of the stadium, rumblings to change the name began. "Broncos Stadium" would have been improper; the AAA Bears still called it home and played ten times as many games there per year. "DOERS Stadium" was proposed. But ultimately, all parties settled on a name that would become iconic ... "Denver Mile High Stadium."

"Denver? Where the Hell Is That?"

Beyond the legitimacy conferred by the Broncos' looming ascension to the NFL was the notion that for the first time since 1960—when the AFL's drafting was in part based on territories parceled to each team—the Broncos could count on seeing their No. 1 draft pick in uniform that following season.

But that didn't necessarily mean the man they picked would want the job.

"I almost died," Floyd Little recalled decades later. "It was not what I expected. I was halfway not happy about it because I had talked with the (New York) Jets and I had to get to the ninth pick in order to go with the Jets. I had also spoken with Jim Finks, who was on his way to Minnesota, and I also spoke with (Vince) Lombardi who had an interest in drafting me (for the Packers), but I told him I was already committed to go to the Jets.

"The only way I got to Denver was because of our Sports Information Director at Syracuse, Val Pinchbeck. Lou Saban had decided to draft Gene Upshaw and then he asked Val what kind of guy Floyd Little is. Val told him that I was a good guy, but said he knew the Broncos were going to draft Upshaw. Saban said, 'Well, we are going to draft Floyd Little.' That is how I got to Denver."

The call stunned him.

"When I got the call I was expecting a call from (Jets head coach) Weeb Eubank, but instead there was this guy with a real deep voice who said, 'Hey, Floyd, Lou Saban with the Denver Broncos. We just drafted you number one, what do you think about that?' I said, 'Denver, where the hell is that?' So, no, I was not happy.

"Then I came to visit in April sometime and the weather was absolutely gorgeous and I fell in love with Denver. Growing up on the East Coast I never really knew where Denver was other than the history and the (covered) wagons were traveling through on the way to the gold rush. But I didn't know where Denver was. I wasn't happy when I was drafted by Denver, but I was happy that I was (drafted) and it turned out very well."

When Little arrived, he discovered a city ready to fall in love with him. Although he didn't win the Heisman Trophy in 1966 at Syracuse University, he was arguably the most prominent player in college football that season. He wore the famed No. 44 for the Orangemen, donning the jersey made famous by Jim Brown and Ernie Davis in the previous decade.

Then he spent the next nine seasons making No. 44 as famous in Colorado as it was in upstate New York. Denver fell head over heels for Little, and the city is still in love with the first superstar Bronco.

Lou Saban Steps In

Little's arrival was only part of the overall reinvigoration of the franchise in 1967. The man who drafted him, coach and general manager Lou Saban, was perceived of equal, if not greater, importance to legitimizing the Broncos as they prepared to move into the NFL.

Saban brought a championship pedigree: the 1964 AFL Championship Game win he directed with the Buffalo Bills remains the last time that club won the biggest prize available to it. But the fact that the Broncos hired Saban after a one-year sojourn to the University of Maryland revealed a restless streak that defined him as a coach. Before there was the peripatetic Larry Brown in basketball, there was Saban, setting the standard for job-hopping. (Appropriately, both passed through Denver within a decade of each other, and both stayed five years—well above their career averages.)

Saban had left the Bills after 1965, saying there were no more mountains to conquer there. He came to Denver and laid eyes on an entire range of them—literally and figuratively. Any team-related accomplishment of note for the Broncos would be a franchise first.

He signed a ten-year contract as head coach and general manager. He stipulated that he wouldn't take the job without a new facility and practice fields on which his team could train, so after seven years in the Quonset hut, the Broncos finally moved to larger digs at 5700 Logan Street, in the industrial north side of town.

"Your main goal is to instill the winning habit as soon as possible," Saban proclaimed. "Bronco fans have been patient, but patience is a bad word."

But it was one they would need to continue using. Although Little excited the fans, the roster was overhauled. Perennial All-AFL offensive tackle Eldon Danenhauer retired. Future Ring of Fame safety Goose Gonsoulin was waived. Lionel Taylor was traded to the Raiders. Those moves were justifiable, or unpreventable. But the one the Broncos would have loved to have had back was when Saban sent cornerback Willie Brown to Oakland along with quarterback Mickey Slaughter in exchange for defensive tackle Rex Mirich and a third-round pick. Brown was already an All-AFL cornerback who had fourteen interceptions in the previous three years and would terrorize Broncos receivers twice a year for the next decade.

Saban pinned his hopes on youth. Thirteen of the Broncos' twenty-two starters early in the season were rookies or second-year players, including Little, and at one point in the season, thirty-two of forty players on the roster were rookies or second-year players. There was so much roster shuffling that at times, the new headquarters resembled the bustling hub terminal at Denver's Stapleton Airport.

But Saban had more riding on quarterback Steve Tensi than anyone else, having sent the Broncos' first-round picks in 1968 and 1969 to the Chargers in the off-season for the twenty-four–year-old passer.

One of those picks was Marty Domres, who never established himself as a starting pro quarterback. But another was lineman Russ Washington, who was a fifteen-year starter and five-time Pro Bowler for the Chargers, beginning his career as a defensive tackle before moving to offense, where he became a boulder of a right tackle protecting Hall of Famer Dan Fouts.

A blocker like Washington could have helped Tensi, who spent much of his time in Denver running for his life behind an offensive line that leaked pass rushers —an all-too-common trait of the 1960s Broncos.

MARLIN THE MAGICIAN

Always under siege, Tensi struggled with injuries during his Broncos tenure. Early in the 1968 season, he fractured his collarbone. The second-teamer, Joe DiVito, failed to consistently move the team. With no other options on hand, Saban inserted a 14th-round pick into the lineup late in the Broncos' third regular-season game.

But Marlin Briscoe was more than just a late-round pick from a small football program (Nebraska-Omaha)—he was the first African-American quarterback to play and start in the American Football League.

"As far as being black, white, pink or blue, it didn't make a difference," Saban later said. "Here was a talent that could electrify the fans and the team itself that surrounded him enjoyed seeing the things he was doing."

With a strong arm and quick feet, Briscoe was a power surge to a team that needed it, running for a touchdown that narrowed the gap against Boston to 20-17. The Broncos lost by that score, but Briscoe won the fans' hearts, and he finished the season with 14 passing touchdowns and three rushing touchdowns. His completion percentage was low (41.5), but not the lowest in the AFL. Besides, this was an era where 47.5 percent of all passes were completed; Briscoe's season was promising.

But, Saban had no intention of making him the full-time quarterback. Upon learning he would be a backup the next year with Tensi returning, Briscoe asked for his release, and it was granted. At his next stop, the Bills converted him to wide receiver, and it was a wise move; he was an All-Pro by 1970 and earned two Super Bowl rings with the Miami Dolphins playing the position. He would also play for the San Diego Chargers, Detroit Lions, and New England Patriots before retiring after the 1976 season. Briscoe threw just nine regular-season passes in his eight years after leaving the Broncos. He caught 224 for 3,537 yards and 30 touchdowns.

By the time Briscoe retired, other African-American quarterbacks had led NFL teams—Joe Gilliam in Pittsburgh and James Harris in Los Angeles. But the deserved opportunities still weren't there. Lamentably, change came—although it was glacial. But Briscoe will always have a place in pro football history, breaking a barrier that never should have been erected in the first place.

MT. SABAN AND THE OCCASIONAL ERUPTION

One reason why Saban wore out his welcome in so many stops was his volcanic emotions. On the sideline, Saban ran on a jagged edge between love for his players and verbal destruction.

Saban's temper and wild emotional swings were on display often in his NFL coaching career. One moment that will likely be associated with him until the end of American football came when NFL Films fitted him with a wireless microphone for a game against the Houston Oilers on November 16, 1969.

The game wasn't memorable—except for the fact that the Broncos blew a 20-3 lead and settled for a 20-20 tie that dropped them to 4-5-1. But Saban's exclamations live on, including two in particular:

"My daughter could do better!"

... and, of course ...

"They're killing me, Whitey; they're killing me!"

"Whitey" was assistant coach Whitey Dovell, a football lifer that Saban had brought with him from Maryland. A decade later, after leaving the Broncos, he would return to the staff. Two decades later, he would be one of the central figures in the revival of the arch-rival Kansas City Chiefs as their director of player personnel, for whom he was still working when he died of cancer, aged sixty-five, in 1992. But despite Dovell's lengthy resume, he went into history as the answer to a football trivia question: "Just who was 'Whitey'?"

Whitey was a man who, like the rest of the coaching staff, couldn't control a force of nature like Saban.

"He just fired guys during the game," Little recalled. "He fired the kickoff team at halftime in Houston when we played at old Rice Stadium. He challenged all of our players when we played an exhibition game in Utah. He was a wild man because he was a player for Cleveland and he was very competitive and he wanted to win."

And with forty-two seconds remaining in a 34-32 win over Buffalo on November 24, 1968, Saban even fired Little.

"We're two points ahead (31-29), running out the clock," Little said. "Lou says, 'Just keep in bounds.' I run a sweep and I don't know why, but I fumbled the ball.

"(Buffalo's George Saimes) advanced it, I got off the ground and tackled him. I come over to the sideline and Coach says, 'You're done.'

So I go toward the locker room. Then, I decided I'm not going to end my career that way."

The Bills had taken the lead on an 18-yard field goal with 30 seconds left. A five-second kickoff return later, the Broncos had the football at their 31-yard-line, and Little strolled back into the game.

"I went back in the huddle and Coach is screaming at me," Little recalled in 2010 before he was inducted into the Pro Football Hall of Fame. "I give him the old, 'Up yours' and said, 'I ain't leaving.' Marlin Briscoe's the quarterback. I said, 'Marlin, throw the ball as far as you can straight down the field.'

"I see this pass coming. I go up over these great defenders—John Pitts, George Saimes, George Byrd—and I get the ball."

Fifty-nine yards later, Little was brought down at the Buffalo 10-yard-line. A Bills face mask penalty moved the football to the 5, and from there, Bobby Howfield kicked the game-winning, 12-yard field goal.

"Coach comes over and says 'I'm going to give you one more week,'" Little recalled. Of course, Little would never play in a uniform other than Denver's and the stage was set for him to become the first Broncos legend.

Despite the contentiousness, Little and Saban grew close through the decades and remained in contact until Saban died in 2009. Saban didn't stop coaching until he left Chowan University in Murfreesboro, North Carolina, at the age of eighty-one after two seasons.

"He was an intense person, but I loved him," Little said. "Even though he fired me and we had our words, we got along pretty well together. I enjoyed playing for Lou and I think anyone who played for him would say the same. He was easy to work for and if you put out the effort and gave it your all, he would respect that and put his arms around you and say, 'You did the best you could, my friend.' That is the kind of coach he was. I loved Lou Saban."

Saban's whistle-stop tour after Denver through all levels of football ultimately included three high schools in the 1980s, West Point, the University of Miami, the New York Yankees (as team president), three small colleges, a semi-pro side called the Middle Georgia Heat Wave, and, for barely a month, the Arena Football League's Milwaukee Mustangs, who fired him after an 0-4 start. When he was the University of Central Florida's head coach from 1982 to 1984, he was called "Lou 'Two-Point-Two' Saban," because the average length of his jobs was 2.2 years.

"I have been known as a peripatetic coach," Saban said in 1994. "The first time I heard that, I thought it was a dirty word."

By comparison, Saban's tenure with the Broncos lasted an eternity: five full years, although he handed off the coaching duties to Jerry Smith and kept the general manager responsibilities midway through 1971, his last season.

As the 1960s ended, Saban's Broncos were inching forward. In 1969, they defeated Joe Namath and the defending Super Bowl champion Jets at home in Week 2, and stood at 4-4 in early November before losing four of their next five games. Tickets were moving at a brisk pace. The AFL was legitimizing itself with back-to-back Super Bowl wins, and as the Broncos moved to the massive, 26-team NFL, the leagues had achieved parity—and Denver had big-league status.

But after fighting to establish and save the franchise in the first decade, the Broncos and their fans would want much more in the years to come—starting with that first winning season.

CHAPTER TWO

The 1970s

As the Broncos' second decade began, Lou Saban had not exhausted the reservoir of credibility and fan goodwill he carried with him from Buffalo. Floyd Little was everything the Broncos had hoped he would be; had he not suffered a late-season knee injury, he would have likely led pro football in rushing yardage and his 5.0-yards-per-carry average made him the most potent ground threat Denver had ever possessed. And even though Steve Tensi had never flourished enough to seize the job Saban was cobbling together a decent collection of talent, with future Ring of Famers Rich Jackson at defensive end and Billy Thompson at cornerback. Each of Saban's first three seasons had seen incremental improvement, from 3-11 in 1967 to 5-9 in 1968 and 5-8-1 a year later. Even the uniforms had changed; the iconic "D" with a horse was introduced in 1968 and would have a longer reign than any Broncos logo to date.

But the AFL-NFL merger created new divisions and thrust the Broncos into treacherous waters. Denver's placement in the AFC West meant that the road to the playoffs went through defending world champion Kansas City and perennially powerful Oakland. Then, as now, the Broncos needed a passing game that was a legitimate threat; without one, they wouldn't overcome a pair of Super Bowl quarterbacks in the Chiefs' Len Dawson and Raiders' Daryle Lamonica.

BREAD AND CIRCUSES

As the 1971 season began, Saban was only four years into his ten-year contract. But after 1970 brought a free-fall from a 4-1 start to a 5-8-1 finish, there was discontent. He still hadn't solved the conundrum at quarterback, and after starting Steve Tensi, Pete Liske, and Al Pastrana in 1970, settled on former Packers quarterback Don Horn in 1971, trading for him in a deal that involved swapping first-round picks in the 1972 draft.

Horn was adequate, but the defense was improving, and on a chilly 49-degree afternoon in Week 1, it accounted for three takeaways: two forced fumbles and an interception. Miami fumbled twice more on interception and punt returns, and kicker Garo Yepremian missed two field-goal attempts.

The final fumble on a mishandled punt return by Jake Scott was recovered by Bobby Anderson; the turnover gave the Broncos first-and-10 at their 23-yard-line with 1:14 remaining. Enough time for Horn to throw, to send Little out on the kind of pass pattern he ran three years earlier against Buffalo when the Broncos were down by one point in the last minute.

Instead, Horn handed off to Little three consecutive times. Only after Little got out of bounds with 27 seconds left at the Denver 38 did Saban send in a pass call; and Horn quickly found Anderson for 12 yards. But with 19 seconds remaining, there was no margin for error, since Little's three runs had gobbled up 47 seconds of clock time. When the Broncos took a 15-yard penalty on the next play, the 10-all draw was assured.

Boos engulfed the Broncos as they left the field, and all were directed at the head coach. But Saban had some logical reasons for playing it tight late in the game. The dirt infield for baseball at Mile High Stadium had not been covered with grass for the fall, and footing was treacherous. And prior to Anderson's fumble recovery, the offense had gone three-and-out and Horn had slipped while trying to throw, resulting in a 9-yard loss that effectively ended the drive.

"We tried to lose it once, and I wasn't going to let us give it away at the end by trying to throw from deep in our own territory—especially when we had to throw out of the muck," Saban said.

All things considered, a tie was a good result given the opposition. The Dolphins were at the precipice of a dynasty. They made the postseason the year before under recently hired coach Don Shula and would represent the AFC in the next three Super Bowls, winning two.

But no one cared about the Dolphins' pedigree after Saban uttered the words that doomed him in Denver:

"It's an old saying, but I'd rather have half a loaf than none."

These were not the words that could assuage an angry fan base. And they were not the words his team wanted to hear, either.

"He said that if I didn't run the clock out, I wouldn't play the rest of the season," Horn told *The Denver Post* in 2012. "Settling for the tie was deflating to the whole team."

Two weeks later, the Broncos returned to Mile High Stadium, having lost to the Green Bay Packers in Milwaukee in the interim. Fans brandished half-loaves of bread as the Broncos fell to the Chiefs, 16-3.

By 1974, the strategy of settling for a tie was forgotten, replaced by a 15-minute, sudden-death overtime to break deadlocks. In the last four seasons before regular-season sudden death, twenty-nine games ended in ties. But in 1971, it doomed Saban.

FAN FURY

Fan discord mushroomed through the rest of the season. The supporters had been patient through Saban's rebuilding project and the losing seasons that preceded it, and the Broncos' long non-strike sellout streak that continues to this day began with the first game of the 1970 season. Denver and the Front Range were doing their part to support the team.

But now, they were fed up. Broncos fans wanted some return on their financial and emotional investment.

"You can't believe the things they call us and the things they throw at us," center Larry Kaminski told *Sports Illustrated* during the season. "I do some public relations work for the club, and I would try to tell people that it was because of injuries, but they didn't pay any attention. One guy listened to me, then he said, 'If I pay 50 cents for a bottle of milk, I expect a good bottle of milk. And when I pay $7.50 for a football ticket, I expect a good football game.'"

They got good football games—but not enough Broncos wins. The heroics at Mile High Stadium too often belonged to the visitors, such as when forty-three-year-old George Blanda led one of his series of dramatic comeback wins for the Raiders during the 1970 season, throwing a late 20-yard touchdown pass to Fred Biletnikoff that dropped Denver to 4-5 and virtually ended their postseason hopes in 1970.

Ten months later, the environment was growing toxic. Saban knew he was nearly out of time.

Polish Night Out

The Broncos were 1-3-1 by the time they went to Cleveland to face the Browns for the first time on October 24, 1971. The Broncos still had never had a winning season; the Browns had not endured a losing season since four years before the Broncos were born, and en route to their sixth postseason game in eight years.

The result was the most dominant performance of the Saban era: a 27-0 thrashing. The Broncos won with efficient, if infrequent, passing from Don Horn (eight completions in sixteen attempts, 85 yards and a touchdown); strong running from Bobby Anderson and Floyd Little, who combined for 184 yards; and three interceptions: one each by Billy Thompson, Chip Myrtle, and Fred Forsberg. Denver amassed 365 total yards and held the Browns to just 60.

But there was something else: the meal the night before the game was organized by Kaminski, a Cleveland native. Kaminski was injured, but made the trip and took his teammates for some Polish home cooking.

"We had kielbasa, stuffed cabbage, and city chicken, and they loved it," Kaminski said after the game. "I guess it gave them a little more energy today, too."

"City chicken" included nothing resembling chicken; it's a dish popularized in Midwest industrial cities in which cubes of pork are placed on a skewer, then fried. But no matter what it was, it agreed with the Broncos, who temporarily squelched the building discontent with the win.

It also meant something more to the Broncos: it embarrassed Cleveland owner Art Modell. During the AFL-NFL merger negotiations in 1966, Modell proclaimed, "I don't ever want to see the Denver Broncos play in my stadium." As the years would prove, the history of his franchise would have been far different had his wish been granted; the Broncos went 8-2 at Municipal Stadium, including one of the most famous wins in team history: the 1986 AFC Championship Game highlighted by "The Drive."

Saban's End, and a New Era Dawns

But the win in Cleveland was Saban's last as Broncos head coach. The Broncos had a winnable stretch afterward, but could not build on the Browns win and lost their next three games to clubs that went a combined 17-23-2. Saban resigned as head coach after that, ceding the job to Jerry Smith while announcing his intent to remain as general manager.

By late December 1971, he'd resigned from that job as well. Saban returned to the Buffalo Bills, which he left in 1965 after lamenting that there were no more mountains to conquer. After failing to scale the peaks in the Rockies, he returned to the period of his greatest success, and he would win again. Saban had upgraded the talent in Denver, but the results were numbingly familiar.

After Smith went 2-3 as interim head coach, the Broncos moved on. But Saban would return to Denver, leading the Bills into Mile High Stadium for a preseason game in 1973. Fans had not forgotten and greeted Saban and the Bills with another shower of half-loaves of bread.

The end of the 1971 season didn't just lead to a change in the coaching staff but for a moment, change at running back was a possibility. Little, the franchise touchstone who had grown close to Saban, admitted late in the season that he could be playing his last season.

"I originally planned to play five years, and this is the end of my fifth," Little said as the season wound down.

But he came back in 1972—and did so as the league's rushing champion, having gained 1,133 yards the previous season and becoming the first Bronco runner to ever hit four figures. His return was a blessing for John Ralston, the Stanford University head coach who assumed the dual head coach/general manager role on Jan. 5. He signed a five-year contract for a substantial raise over his previous salary and went to work.

It didn't take long for Broncos players to notice a difference.

"Lou expected you to be able to adjust to little things without being very explicit about them. John will take more time for everything. He's very precise," offensive tackle Mike Current told *Sports Illustrated* during Ralston's first preseason as Broncos coach. "We've been treated more like college players than pros. In many cases it's been good because we got back to some fundamentals, but a lot of the players have resented the little things. The more I see of John Ralston, the more he reminds me of Woody Hayes. He's not as obstinate and overbearing, but things are going to be done his way."

The attention to detail marked the biggest adjustment, and to install this, Ralston led the Broncos out of Colorado for training camp. Ralston's first four camps would be held at the Cal Poly Pomona campus; prior to this, the team had trained at the Colorado School of Mines in Golden, Colorado State University in Fort Collins, or at the new headquarters to which the team moved in 1967, Saban's first year.

During that training camp, Ralston received the most important player endorsement: from Little.

""He's got a pretty good approach: Get everyone tired and leaning on each other. It creates unity, and a little more of that won't hurt us." Little said at the time.

WELL-SPOKEN VS. MR. MALAPROP

Ralston was a good fit for a job that had some college-like characteristics, particularly the need to engage a supporter base that felt invested in the team after the Save-the-Broncos efforts of the 1960's. He was also a clear communicator. The polar opposite of Ralston was Bill Peterson, a successful coach at Florida State in spite of spewing a dizzying array of mixed metaphors and malapropisms. Both entered the NFL in 1972 to much fanfare and made their debuts against each other on September 17 at Mile High Stadium, when the Broncos faced the Oilers.

The similarities stopped there.

On one game day, Peterson asked if a player would lead the team in saying the Lord's Prayer. When no one raised his hand, Peterson said it himself. He gathered the team and opened with, "Now I lay me down to sleep ... " He didn't know every player's name. He asked his players to pair off in groups of three.

Unsurprisingly, the Broncos won 30-17 in front of an enthusiastic crowd of 51,656 that set a then-Broncos record. Little ran twenty-two times for 101 yards. Six different Broncos defenders sacked Houston quarterback Dan Pastorini.

JOHN RALSTON AND THE ERA OF GOOD FEELINGS

Ralston's style upon his arrival was a 180-degree pivot from Saban's. Instead of tempestuous reactions, Ralston bubbled optimism.

A certified Dale Carnegie instructor, Ralston wanted to change the organizational culture by force of personality. Every day was about "getting better." It wasn't a matter of *if* the Broncos would improve, but when, and he boldly proclaimed that the Broncos would finish the 1972 season 10-4.

"You don't fake this sort of thing," he told *Sports Illustrated* in 1973. "If you put up a false facade of positive thinking, people will see through it. I'm just this way all the time."

Then the Broncos exhausted that quantity of defeats in the four weeks after the win over Houston, hitting loss No. 4 with an excruciating 23-20 loss to the Vikings in which Denver conceded a game-winning Fran Tarkenton-to-Gene Washington touchdown pass with just seventeen seconds remaining. Ralston was unfazed.

His sentiment was justified a week later when the Broncos marched into Oakland and defeated the Raiders 30-23. It snapped a 14-game Raiders win streak in the series that dated back to 1965 and was the Broncos' first win there in a decade.

It wasn't a coincidence that the game was Charley Johnson's first as the Broncos' starting quarterback.

CHARLEY JOHNSON STEADIES THE SHIP

The Broncos' futile search for a franchise passer after Frank Tripucka's final retirement was a root cause of the team's inability to even hit .500 after getting there in 1962. It took a PhD to stop this cycle—literally, because Johnson is Dr. Charles Johnson, having earned his doctorate from Washington University in St. Louis in 1971. He played for the St. Louis Cardinals from 1961 to 1969 and the Houston Oilers the following two seasons before Ralston acquired him for a third-round pick.

It was a small price to pay for someone who profoundly changed the Broncos. Johnson didn't start his first five games as Bronco; that distinction belonged to Steve Ramsey, a holdover from the Saban era who also started the last five games of 1971. But with the offense struggling against the Vikings on October 15, 1972, Ralston inserted Johnson.

"He taught us how to win," wide receiver Haven Moses would later recall.

The Broncos fell short against Minnesota, but at Oakland the next week, Johnson completed 20 of 28 passes for 361 yards and two touchdowns as the Broncos built a 24-3 lead and held on for the 30-23 win. It would be the first of twenty-seven consecutive starts for Johnson, who held down the position for all but two games until the accumulation of injuries began to catch up with him midway through the 1975 season.

"Before the game, they would stand him up on a table and tape him from head to toe. We called him 'The Mummy,'" Moses later recalled. "His body had been ravaged over time. But he was a smart quarterback. He was a very patient quarterback."

Johnson retired after the 1975 season widely considered the best Broncos quarterback to that point, and his role in the Ralston revival helped ensure his eventual inclusion in the Broncos' Ring of Fame.

MONDAY NIGHT MADNESS

*M*onday Night Football had been on the air for three-plus seasons before the Broncos finally got their turn in the spotlight. By the time ABC and its traveling circus made it to Mile High Stadium, *MNF* had become a pop-cultural phenomenon. Even the halftime highlights, narrated by the irascibly eloquent Howard Cosell, were scrutinized, and fans of low-wattage teams—including Denver—complained vociferously when their sides were left out of the package.

Even though the Broncos had not broken past .500, their progress in Ralston's first season was sufficient to merit a treasured spot. On October 22, a national television audience—a good chunk of which was barely familiar with the Broncos—would find out how Ralston's construction project was faring.

What would be a better opponent than the Raiders? And who better to introduce the event than "Dandy" Don Meredith, who appeared to predict a change in Colorado laws forty years in the future when he proclaimed, "Welcome to the Mile High City—and I really am!"

"It was the Raiders, the 'Evil Empire,' coming to town. It was Howard coming to town. It was all of that orange," said kicker Jim Turner when he reflected on the game to *The Denver Post* in 2000. "And we also just happened to be a pretty good football team."

But by the end of the game, it wasn't Meredith's warbling or Cosell's intonations that owned the night, but Johnson and Little. Together, they led the Broncos on a last-minute drive after the Raiders had taken the lead with thirty-six seconds remaining on a 49-yard George Blanda field goal. After taking possession at the Denver 38-yard-line following a pair of kickoffs that went out of bounds and a 25-yard return by Joe Dawkins, Johnson hit Little for 13 yards, handed off to Dawkins for 12 more and then to Little for 9 yards. Turner then sent the 35-yard field-goal attempt through the north uprights with three seconds remaining.

"I was really, really good friends with George Blanda," Turner said years later. "But after that game, he wouldn't even talk to me. He figured I'd stole his show."

Two years after the infamous "half a loaf" game, the Broncos had a far more satisfying tie, as delicious as a steak dinner. Instead of killing morale, it raised it. The Broncos went undefeated in their next five games, winning four and tying one, to move to 6-3-2. A win at San Diego sealed the franchise's first winning season, and the Broncos finished 7-5-2 and finally with something to show for Ralston's perpetual optimism.

THE FIRST OVERTIME

R ules changes have been a part of the NFL for decades, and 1974 brought some of the most radical alterations to the game. The goalposts were moved from the goal line to the back of the end zone, kickoffs were moved from the 40-yard-line to the 35, offensive holding penalties were cut from 15 to 10 yards, and sudden-death overtime was introduced to regular-season play.

Having never played in the postseason, the Broncos had never experienced sudden death. It didn't take them long, as they and the Steelers became the first teams to play a regular-season overtime period … which did nothing to change the result. Both teams squandered opportunities and the 35-35 final was exactly the kind of result that regular-season sudden death was designed to prevent.

The same teams would take another step in the evolution of overtime thirty-seven years and four months later, when they met in the AFC wild-card playoffs on January 8, 2012. By then, the rules had changed for the postseason, mandating at least one possession for each team—unless the team that opened overtime with the football drove to a touchdown. That was exactly what happened; Tim Tebow hit Demaryius Thomas in stride for an 80-yard touchdown pass on the first play of the extra session, and the new rules were never tested; it was sudden death, as it had been under the old rules.

STRAIGHT OUTTA YANKTON

A small college in South Dakota seemed the most unlikely place to find a man who was perhaps the wildest Bronco to ever suit up. But nothing about defensive end Lyle Alzado was normal, considering that one of his most notable undergraduate accomplishments was winning the school's pie-eating championship.

While growing up in Brooklyn, New York, Alzado brawled and flirted with legal trouble. As he grew older, he boxed in the Police Athletic League; at one point, he won twenty-seven consecutive bouts. He flourished at football but was a poor student. He only had one scholarship offer, and it was revoked, sending him on a path through junior college in Texas before he ended up at Yankton, where he put on weight and found his callings: as a Little All-American defensive lineman and in working with children, majoring in physical education.

Long-time Broncos assistant Stan Jones discovered Alzado, and Saban selected Alzado with the first of the Broncos' two fourth-round selections in the 1971 draft. He was an immediate starter after veteran Pete Duranko suffered a season-ending ankle injury.

"He was a coach's dream and a coach's nightmare, both at the same time," long-time defensive coordinator Joe Collier later said of Alzado. "Everybody's had their characters. But for me, there will never be another guy like him. He was a difficult guy to coach. But once he strapped on the helmet on Sunday, he was a great guy to coach."

He was also one of the Broncos' most community-minded players. He invested countless hours contributing to myriad charities and school systems, speaking and volunteering. And no one was more thankful for the chance he'd been given.

"I owe everything to football," Alzado told *Sports Illustrated* during the 1977 season. ""How else could I be known everywhere I go? People treat you like you're the President or something if you're a football player. It's ridiculous. Without football I'd probably be dealing dope on a street corner or sitting in a jail somewhere."

Football saved his life, and he became a larger-than-life personality, only growing in stature after moving on to Cleveland and then to the Los Angeles Raiders. Eventually, he dabbled in acting. At one point, he returned to his roots by boxing Muhammad Ali in an exhibition match at Mile High Stadium in July 1979.

But he believed the sport, and the measures he took to succeed in it, indirectly killed him. Alzado died of brain cancer in 1992, and attributed the illness to steroids he took during his playing days. Although no link had been established between steroid use and brain cancer, Alzado passionately spoke against steroids in his final months, directing his anti-drug messages toward children. Once more, the passions that Alzado cultivated at Yankton came to the forefront.

BACK TO THE BALLOT BOX

It wasn't the threat of relocation that spurred the successful campaign to expand Mile High Stadium in 1974, but the demand. Every game in the 1970s was a sellout, and the waiting list for season tickets continued to grow. Denver was also growing as a viable sports market; the American Basketball Association's Nuggets were starting to thrive, and rumblings of National Hockey League and Major League Baseball franchises continued in the distance.

By 1976, construction to expand Mile High Stadium was well under way. The north end zone would have two upper decks to match the west stands, and the east stands would be reconstructed as a three-decked structure to match the other two stands. That grandstand was an engineering model; it weighed 4,500 tons and could be hydraulically moved 145 feet forward for the football configuration, and then back for baseball. It took approximately six hours for the stands to be put into position for one sport or the other.

Sports in Denver were booming. McNichols Sports Arena had opened a bounce pass south of Mile High Stadium; its construction helped pave the path for the Nuggets' move to the National Basketball Association upon the ABA's demise. The NHL arrived the same year when the Kansas City Scouts moved to Denver, changing their name to the Colorado Rockies.

But the Broncos, above the others, held Denver under their spell. The first stage of Mile High's $25 million expansion was completed by the 1976 season and another round of attendance records fell, with home crowds pushing over 60,000 for the first time.

FLOYD LITTLE'S PERFECT ENDING

But as the stadium rose again, Little's workload had decreased as time and the accumulation of hits caught up with him by the mid-1970s. More carries went to younger contributors like Otis Armstrong and Jon Keyworth. By 1975, Little was reduced to a secondary role—which was underscored by the player the club chose to put on the cover of its media guide: Armstrong. Little usually started, but touched the football an average of eleven times a game. All the while, he remained remarkably durable, and finished his career by playing in 86 consecutive games.

But after nine seasons, he knew it was time to walk away, announcing that 1975 would be his final season. Little would never get the chance to lead the Broncos to the postseason; when the Philadelphia Eagles arrived for the home finale on December 14, the Broncos were 5-7, having never recovered from a midseason tailspin in which they lost five of six games.

The hapless Eagles had managed to tie the game at 10-apiece in the third quarter. Conditions were brutal; it was 18 degrees, and 15,000 ticket-holders had not bothered to show up. Frustration set in from the sideline to the last row of the south stands.

At this point, Little seized control. Following the game-tying field goal, the Broncos assumed possession at their 34-yard-line with 1:45 left in the third quarter, and Little spoke up.

"Everybody get somebody; I'm going to take it the distance."

Ramsey called a swing pass. Little caught it at the Denver 42 and moved as if fired from a cannon, darting through Philadelphia defenders as though they were traffic cones. For one moment, this was the Little of the early 1970s, and he didn't stop until reaching the end zone with a 66-yard catch-and-run to give the Broncos the lead for good.

"Honest to God, it was kind of like Babe Ruth (calling his shot)," said Ramsey.

And Little was not done. Offensive coordinator Max Coley called Little's number ten more times on passes and handoffs. On the first play after the two-minute warning, he sprinted untouched off right tackle into the end zone for the game-clinching touchdown.

Little's curtain call for the home fans was a masterpiece: two touchdowns and 150 yards from scrimmage. He was carried off the field by jubilant, grateful fans who stormed out of the stands to fete their conquering hero. Later, he left Mile High Stadium in a limousine, which Charley Johnson and his teammates had arranged to take Little and his wife to a party organized in his honor.

"If I could have drawn it up, it couldn't have been any better," Little said.

On the opposite sideline, Eagles coach Mike McCormack watched the proceedings with profound respect, saying, "I would like to have 43 Floyd Littles."

His legend in Denver was secure. No Bronco would ever wear jersey No. 44 again; it joined Frank Tripucka's No. 18 among uniforms taken out of circulation. But it would take thirty-five years for Little's recognition to go beyond Colorado, when he finally made the Pro Football Hall of Fame.

By that time, he had long since passed through the primary nomination process and went through the Seniors Committee. The diligent work of fan and author Tom Mackie and then *Denver Post* reporter Jeff Legwold helped build Little's case. The meticulous Legwold reviewed each of Little's carries and found that he was hit behind the line of scrimmage on approximately 30 percent of them, evidence of the issues along the Broncos' offensive line during Little's career.

No other teammate of Little's—or late 1960s or 1970s Bronco, period—is in the Pro Football Hall of Fame. The Orange Crush remains unrepresented. From the pre-Little years, only cornerback Willie Brown has a bust in Canton, and he is remembered more for his twelve seasons as an Oakland Raider—"Old Man Willie," as legendary Raiders broadcaster Bill King famously proclaimed—than his four years in Denver.

"There are a ton of players that are certainly deserving and I think Randy Gradishar is that guy. I think Billy Thompson is that guy. I think Louis Wright is that guy. I think Rick Jackson is that guy," Little said, adding linebacker Tom Jackson as another Bronco deserving of induction. "These guys were football players. They played on teams that weren't very good teams and yet they were good players and when you look at what they've done in their lives and what they've done as players ..."

Little trailed off, but his point was—and remains—clear. The Broncos have played in eight Super Bowls and won three, and have just seven Hall of Famers—two of whom were known more for their exploits elsewhere. The Kansas City Chiefs have played in two Super Bowls, winning one, and have eighteen Hall of Famers, including fourteen who played, coached, or administrated at least five seasons for that club.

But for now, the Ring of Fame will have to do for these Broncos legends. Meanwhile, Hall-of-Famers Little, Gary Zimmerman, John Elway, Shannon Sharpe, and Terrell Davis wait for company to arrive.

RISE OF THE ORANGE CRUSH

Joe Collier had been the Broncos' defensive coordinator since 1972, having been promoted from defensive backs coach by Ralston. Collier had been with the Broncos since 1969, joining the club that year after three years as Buffalo's head coach where he was Saban's successor. But it wasn't until his defense began collecting future stars that he was able to do what he wanted.

In 1973, Ralston picked Louisville linebacker Tom Jackson in the fourth round. He became a full-time starter by 1974 and was a defensive linchpin for thirteen more seasons until retiring to pursue a career in broadcasting. Jackson's blossoming was a surprise relative to his draft status, and he remains one of the best mid-round picks in Broncos history.

But the expectations for 1974 first-round pick Randy Gradishar were lofty from the start. His coach at Ohio State, the legendary Woody Hayes, described Gradishar as "the best linebacker I ever coached at Ohio State." Pretty soon, Broncos fans would be describing him as the best linebacker they'd ever seen in a Denver uniform.

"We had a good defense throughout the mid '70s," Collier said in 2002. "We were a bit undersized, but we had the best speed in the league. We were able to run all over the place."

The pieces were falling into place. By the end of 1974, defensive end Barney Chavous was a full-time starter. In 1975, lock-down cornerback Louis Wright burst into the lineup, starting eleven games.

But the final piece of the puzzle was converting to a 3-4 defense on a full-time basis, which happened early in the 1976 season. It was a change dictated by necessity after Lyle Alzado suffered a season-ending knee injury in a Week 1 loss to Cincinnati. It played to the defense's changing strengths, allowing both Joe Rizzo and Bob Swenson to join Jackson and Gradishar in the starting lineup. But the biggest individual beneficiary was Rubin Carter, an unheralded defensive tackle as a rookie who emerged as a terror when pushed to nose tackle in the 3-4 alignment.

Few players have ever been more ideally suited to a position than Carter to playing on the nose. Lining up opposite the opponent's center, he was able to collapse a blocking scheme from inside and occupy multiple blockers, freeing the linebackers to make plays inside and outside. Collier did what great coaches do: he designed a strategy to maximize his players' strengths and minimize their weaknesses, and the defense made a quantum leap.

In the weeks that followed the change, Denver shut out two opponents and allowed just two foes to break 20 points. This was an era of overpowering defenses league-wide, but only the Steelers allowed fewer points in 1976 than the Broncos, who conceded just 14.7 points per game. It was the stingiest of any to that point in Broncos history. The Orange Crush was born.

RUNNING IT UP?

Nine games into the 1976 season, the Broncos played one of their worst halves of the season, and the second half started no better. With four minutes left in the third quarter, they trailed the hapless expansion Tampa Bay Buccaneers, 13-10. It was the first time the Bucs had led in the second half in six weeks and the Broncos were at risk of suffering the biggest upset in their history.

It didn't last. The somnambulant Broncos awoke two snaps after Dave Green's field goal put Tampa Bay in front. Steve Ramsey hit Haven Moses on a deep pass to the Bucs 22, and Dolbin ran the rest of the way to complete a 71-yard touchdown. That sparked one of the biggest outbursts in Broncos history; they scored 38 points in an eight-minute, 33-second span, and walked away with their highest point total since 1963 and the second-biggest margin of victory in club history to that point.

But the action didn't begin until after the final gun, when Bucs coach John McKay refused to shake Ralston's hand. The two coaches had a history dating back to USC-Stanford games in what was then the Pacific-8 Conference, but there was something more to McKay's anger. Afterward, McKay unleashed a fusillade of profanities in accusing Ralston of running up the score, and then challenged Broncos offensive coordinator Max Coley to a fight.

"If he was talking about whipping somebody, he knew where I was dressing," Coley retorted at the time. "I was only about 60 feet away. I learned a long time ago not to get into that particular kind of contest with a skunk. That's the first time I've ever seen a coach blame the other coaching staff for a loss."

It was hard to see how anyone could have possibly blamed the Broncos' position groupings for the score. Of the four touchdowns that came after the Ramsey-to-Moses connection, three were scored by the Denver defense off takeaways. The other score came two plays after Paul Smith sacked Bucs quarterback Steve Spurrier, forcing a fumble that Tom Jackson recovered at the Tampa Bay 17-yard-line. Two plays later—and both were handoffs—the Broncos scored again. After that, Ramsey, the starting quarterback, was pulled in favor of Norris Weese.

"We had all the second-stringers we had left in the game. Maybe he would have liked for us to punt on first down," Coley said. "I don't know who he wanted us to run our offense if not his defensive line—his coaching staff?"

McKay didn't take long to walk back his comments, calling Coley later that week to apologize. But he didn't call Ralston with a similar apology.

"I have been in the other position a lot more than that horse's ass. I don't like any part of him," McKay said of Ralston. "His day is coming."

He had no idea how prescient he would turn out to be.

THE MUTINY OF '76

Ralston had continued to build the talent base on the roster. But the initial misgivings he had about being a coach and a general manager were coming back to the forefront by 1976. Reports of dissension with his coaching style began to circulate. Because he handled the dual role, Ralston had always focused on roster-building and motivation, leaving the tactical details to his coordinators and other assistants.

The Broncos had just posted their best record to that date, a 9-5 mark that was just one game shy of the AFC's lone wild-card berth. The defense was the league's second-best that year, but shaky quarterbacking consigned the Broncos to their 17th consecutive season out of the playoffs. And some players felt that this near miss was as far as Ralston could take them.

In the week after the season ended, some players met among themselves. The group was dubbed "the Dirty Dozen" by some media and its ranks were headlined by a handful of stars: wide receiver Haven Moses, safety Billy Thompson, defensive end Lyle Alzado, running backs Otis Armstrong and Jon Keyworth, and uber-returner Rick Upchurch, who in just two seasons had become the team's most potent big-play threat and one of the league's most dazzling players in the open field.

The following week, they met with owner Gerald Phipps and Fred Gehrke, the long-time executive and former NFL player who assumed the general manager title on December 18, six days after the season ended with a 28-14 win at Chicago. The players wanted to call a press conference to air their grievances, but Gehrke and Phipps talked them out of it. Thompson read a muted statement that offered support for Gehrke and Phipps without mentioning Ralston's name. But an original draft of the players' statement leaked out: "We don't believe it is possible to win a championship under the guidance of John Ralston. He has lost the respect of his players, and we don't believe he is capable of coaching us to a championship."

Ralston dug in.

"I have never walked away from anything in my life, and I'm not a quitter. We've gone too far in the last five years to not see this thing through," Ralston said then. But he added that there was a "strong likelihood that some players will be traded."

Phipps offered a vote of support, stating, "We run the organization. The players don't. Nothing happened to change our opinion of John's coaching abilities." All the while, Ralston was going about his job; when he the statements were made, Ralston was in Montgomery, Alabama, scouting the annual Blue-Gray All-Star Game that took place on Christmas Day.

Ralston went about his work, and made changes of his own. He fired offensive coordinator Max Coley, whose unit had struggled because of the post-Johnson void at quarterback that Steve Ramsey, Norris Weese, and Craig Penrose tried—and largely failed—to fill in 1976.

But behind the scenes, wheels turned, and Gehrke's mind churned.

His perspective on pro football was unique; at various points, he'd played, coached, worked as a broadcaster, tinkered, and designed. He helped design the first full facemask on a helmet, wearing it in 1947. The first helmet logo in the NFL was his design: he painted the Los Angeles Rams' horns on their helmets during the 1948 off-season. Rams owner Dan Reeves—no relation to the eventual Broncos coach—paid Gehrke $1 per helmet for the job. He would retouch the helmets after each game. During his time with the Broncos, which began in 1965, he invented the practice net kickers and punters use on the sideline.

Gehrke was a creative thinker, an idea man. In a copycat league, he took up permanent residence outside the box. And even with discord within the locker room, nudging a coach to the door after the best season in franchise history was as far outside the box as can be imagined.

But in the Broncos' quest to replace Coley, he called a former coworker. Robert "Red" Miller and Gehrke had crossed paths during the 1965 season with the Broncos. Miller was the Broncos' offensive line coach from 1963-65 and Gehrke was the director of player personnel.

Eleven years and a few months later, Gehrke called Miller, then the offensive coordinator of the New England Patriots. He wanted to offer him the same job. Miller declined. He was open to leaving the Patriots, but only to move up.

That chance came a few days later. Ralston faced an awkward situation: he would return, but face something of a demotion, having lost the general manager title. He knew some of his players wanted him fired. On January 31, Ralston resigned. Less than twenty-four hours later, Miller was introduced as the new head coach.

THE RETURN OF "RED"

"I feel I've reached my dream in becoming a head coach in the NFL, and I intend to make the most of it."

—Red Miller, January 31, 1977

Miller could be forgiven for barely recognizing the Broncos franchise when he returned to Denver in 1977 after a dozen years away. When he worked on the staff as an assistant coach from 1963 to 1965, the team was still housed in the Quonset hut, the home stadium was still named for a minor-league baseball team, and the team was run on a tight budget.

But the changes worked both ways. Miller had ascended through the coaching ranks and in 1976 was the offensive coordinator of a Patriots offense that thrived on balance. Three different running backs gained at least 699 yards; all averaged at least 4.1 yards per carry. Mobile quarterback Steve Grogan averaged more yards per carry (6.6) than per pass attempt (6.3) and accounted for 30 touchdowns: 12 rushing and 18 passing. The Patriots scored at least 30 points in half of their fourteen regular-season games in 1976; the Broncos took thirty-one games over three seasons to amass that many 30-plus outputs.

Ralston had lost the faith of his players, but had picked the right ones for his rebuilding project. Never before had the Broncos had the athleticism and football talent that they possessed. Never had the club been run more professionally. And never had the franchise been healthier; with the second and third levels on the north and east stands of Mile High Stadium set for completion, the Broncos had a stadium that seated 75,103—with every seat sold and no-shows scarce.

Unlike when Saban and Ralston arrived, the Broncos didn't need a builder to tear down and reconstruct. They needed a motivator to tinker.

"Instead of rebuilding from a team that was 1-13 or 2-12, as many head coaches must do, my coaches and I inherited a team coming off the most successful season in the history of the franchise," Miller said in 1977. "We had some very talented players. Overall, we had a squad that needed a player here or some improvement there to become a championship team."

It was clear to what position Miller referred when he said "here." With Charley Johnson one year into his retirement, Miller needed a quarterback. No one on the roster was the answer, at least not right away. And that's what mattered. Seventeen years of promises and false dawns were far too many. The Broncos had to win now.

The puzzle only needed one more piece.

A New Leader: Craig Morton

In Denver, the fans were frustrated, but still showered the stars of their home team with adoration. Sixteen hundred miles away in northern New Jersey, fans of the New York Giants were equally peeved with their club's struggles, but channeled their emotions into scorn.

In the mid-1970s, Craig Morton was the object of their derision. The Giants' offense consisted of a hard-working folk hero in running back Doug Kotar, a bunch of wide receivers who struggled to get open, and an offensive line that allowed 93 sacks in two seasons.

"I think people expected too much of Craig Morton," said Andy Robustelli, a Hall of Famer as a player and a Giants executive at the time. "They expected miracles of him, and he didn't give them miracles."

At the same time, Steve Ramsey was trying to establish himself as the Broncos' quarterback. But unlike some of his teammates, he wasn't a star, and took the blame from fans for the team's inability to get over the playoff hump. So when the Broncos and Giants swapped Morton and Ramsey on March 7, 1977, few eyebrows arched at the deal. It appeared on the surface to be a change of scenery for two players who needed it; both were happy about the trade.

"I was disappointed I didn't accomplish what I had set out to accomplish," Morton would recall a year later. "Then after I thought about my being traded, I felt relieved. Relieved to get out of New York."

On the day of the trade, Fred Gehrke declared that Morton would compete for the job with Craig Penrose and Norris Weese, and "give us stability while our two youngsters develop." The deal was portrayed as giving the Broncos a bridge to the future, and most outside of Denver saw it that way.

Prior to joining the Giants, Morton was the starter for the Dallas Cowboys in their Super Bowl V loss to the Baltimore Colts six years earlier. After being pummeled behind the Giants' leaky offensive line the previous three years, most pundits regarded Morton as washed up, figuring his best days were behind him.

But Miller saw that the battered Morton could take a hit and rise back up for the next play. He thought that he could provide Morton an offensive line that gave him just enough time to locate wide receivers Haven Moses and Jack Dolbin downfield. But most of all, Miller believed that Morton could point the way and get his teammates to follow.

"We made the trade because we wanted someone with experience," Miller said. "We wanted something you can't draft. I always felt Craig could throw the ball as well as anyone, and that's what you look for first in a quarterback."

All of that was evident as quickly as the preseason. Although veteran Steve Spurrier was signed and provided a challenge, Morton moved the offense and commanded the huddle, and was named team captain and starter in spite of being a new arrival.

ONE CRUSHING AFTER ANOTHER

B ut it wasn't Morton and the offense that provided the propulsion for the best start in franchise history. Rather it was the defense that defined the 1977 Broncos. A year after learning the 3-4 defense on the fly, the Broncos mastered it as no one did before or since.

In Week 1, defense was all that separated the Broncos from a season-opening loss to the St. Louis Cardinals and their explosive offense. With targets galore, the steady Jim Hart under center, and arguably the best offensive line in the game, the Cardinals had the first pro iteration of the "Air Coryell" attack that Don Coryell would eventually master in San Diego. You didn't shut out this offense. No one had even held it to single digits since 1974.

That the Broncos won wasn't an upset; the Broncos were 9-5 the year before, the Cardinals one game better. The game was at Mile High Stadium, where a then-franchise record 75,002 fans made the newly expanded stands shudder with noise.

But the score was a stunner:

Denver 7, St. Louis 0.

The immovable object had stopped the irresistible force cold. A 10-yard third-quarter touchdown run by Otis Armstrong was all the offense the Broncos needed, capping a modest 34-yard drive set up when St. Louis punter Terry Joyce mishandled a snap.

The defense's fury bled to the special teams. Two of the four field-goal attempts by St. Louis kicker Jim Bakken were deflected, one each by Claudie Minor and Lyle Alzado. The Cardinals had two final chances to tie the game with 1:48 remaining after driving to the Denver 7-yard-line, but a pair of Hart passes fell incomplete.

Morton and the offense still had a long way to go. Plagued by four turnovers, the Broncos averaged just 4.2 yards per play and had as many punts as points. But the defense was becoming an all-timer, and could carry the offense for as long as it took them to adjust to a new coach and quarterback.

Coryell, the offensive mastermind, was convinced.

"I think they're real title contenders," he said.

And title contenders often have the kind of surge that began on September 18, 1977: a six-game winning streak that was the longest in franchise history to that point and saw the Broncos win by an average margin of 14.6 points. The win over St. Louis was the only game in the streak that was close.

The Broncos had arrived.

A NATION TAKES NOTICE

Soon, attention would follow. Four weeks into the streak, copies of that week's *Sports Illustrated* featuring nose tackle Rubin Carter landed in mailboxes. The cover headline read, "The Case for the 3-4 Defense," and featured the third-year ringleader of the Broncos' line staring at readers from behind his face mask, his helmet bearing ample scars of battle.

The Broncos were one of seven teams using the 3-4 defense, but none were more dominant. The choice of Carter for the cover was appropriate: although linebackers Randy Gradishar and Tom Jackson got the headlines, it was Carter and defensive ends Lyle Alzado and Barney Chavous who set them up.

"A nose tackle has to be able to endure the pounding," Carter explained. "On most plays, a 250-pound center and a 260-pound guard hit me. That's 510 pounds each play."

And Carter earned the cover by doing that better than anyone else.

"If just a center can handle our nose tackle, we have no advantage with the 3-4," said defensive coordinator Joe Collier at the time.

"But if the nose man can force a double team, then we have a free linebacker to track down the ball. Rubin's strength is his ability to get away from blocks, meaning the opposition has to double-team him, at least."

Two days after that week's copy of *SI* was in readers' hands, the Broncos flew to the Bay Area for their biggest test to date.

"IT'S ALL OVER, FAT MAN!"

The biggest roadblock on the nascent Broncos' highway to relevance was the defending world champion Raiders, winners of seventeen consecutive games. The vitriol in the rivalry ran only one way at that point. Although the teams had played competitive games in the Ralston era—and the Broncos had even won at Oakland in 1972 and 1974—the Broncos were 2-21-1 against the Raiders dating back to 1965. Oakland had never regarded Denver as a serious threat to their comfortable perch atop the AFC West.

This wasn't the Super Bowl, but it was the closest thing the Broncos franchise had ever witnessed to that point. If you saved a gambit for another day, well, this was the day.

And that set up the greatest trick play in Broncos history. Leading 14-7 with 59 seconds left in the second quarter, Jim Turner lined up for a 42-yard field-goal attempt. But when holder Norris Weese caught the snap, the thirty-six-year-old placekicker mimicked a kick and then sprinted into the left flat.

"I looked first for Riley Odoms," Weese said. "But you can't waste time on the play and I saw Turner wide open and couldn't believe it."

No Raider was within 10 yards. Turner caught the pass at the 16-yard-line and in his trademark black high-top, square-toed kicking shoe, lumbered to the south end zone at Oakland-Alameda County Coliseum, where he was mobbed by teammates.

"I ran into the end zone out of fear. Speed wasn't involved," deadpanned Turner after the game.

Denver cruised from there. Its defense was dominant, rattling Raiders quarterback Ken Stabler into the worst performance of his career, including a nightmarish seven interceptions. Joe Rizzo intercepted three of the passes. Louis Wright intercepted one and returned it 18 yards for a touchdown with 3:45 left in the third quarter to put the game further out of reach.

As the game reached blowout proportions, Tom Jackson turned toward the sideline, looked at John Madden, and bellowed, "It's all over, fat man!" He wasn't talking as much about the game as the Raiders' long-time dominance over the Broncos. The series had become a rivalry. The quote lives on in Broncos lore.

But what is forgotten in the wake of the triumph is what happened a fortnight later: the Raiders flew to Denver and defeated the Broncos, 24-14, ending the Broncos' season-opening streak. Both teams hit midseason at 6-1 and skepticism arose once again about the Broncos. The battle-tested Raiders were expected to pull away in the second half.

Instead, it was the Broncos who kept their poise. They dominated the Pittsburgh Steelers a week later, beating them 21-7 and starting another six-game winning streak. The offense was steady after its opening-week struggles, and Morton was en route to winning AFC Offensive Player of the Year honors. By the time the Broncos lost again, on December 18 to the Cowboys at Texas Stadium in Irving, the AFC West title and No. 1 seed belonged to the Broncos. Most importantly, so did home-field advantage.

Piano Man

"Love" is a strong word for player-coach relationships, but it was easy to see why players loved Miller. He publicly defended them and attempted to keep issues private and out of the media. He didn't burden them with unnecessary rules. And he was willing to subject himself to the same standards as his players.

So when it came time to organize the annual rookie talent show, Miller was asked if a rookie head coach should be a part of the rookie show.

"Get a piano, and the rookie coach will be there," Miller replied.

And with that, Miller went to the piano and belted out some ragtime tunes—after all, the rules applied to him, just like any other Denver newcomer. Who wouldn't want to play for a guy like that?

When "Red" Meant More than Just Hair

Miller was not a sit-in-the-tower coach. He was down on the field, instructing and motivating his players face-to-face rather than through a megaphone from afar.

But during one 1977 practice, that style had a consequence. He wanted to show offensive tackle Claudie Minor proper blocking technique. To do so, he lined up against Minor, a 280-pounder who had nearly 100 pounds on his coach.

At the whistle, Minor rushed at his coach, who blocked. Then the twenty-six-year-old lineman noticed something on Miller's face.

"Coach," Minor said, "You're bleeding. Coach—I'm sorry, Coach, you need the trainer."

Miller didn't care. Red on his head, red on his face, he coached on, refusing to have the cut treated until the job was finished.

FINALLY, THE PLAYOFFS

It was Christmas Eve. As with many days in Denver at that time of year, the sun shone brightly and the air was a bit balmy. And the Broncos were about to give their fans the present for which they had waited since 1960—or whenever they hopped on the bandwagon during the two save-the-team drives that followed: a playoff game. That it would be at Mile High Stadium only made the occasion perfectly sweet; playing the team of the 1970s, the Steelers, made it too good to be true.

By the time the teams kicked off, the Raiders were nearing a double-overtime win over the Baltimore Colts in the early-afternoon divisional-playoff game, ensuring that the Broncos would see their long-time rivals in the AFC Championship if they won. Not that many people outside of the Rocky Mountain region thought such a duel was possible—even though the Steelers had lost 21–7 at Mile High Stadium seven weeks earlier.

"Everybody kept asking all year, 'Are the Broncos for real?'" Thompson said. "That's ended now. People back East don't have to wonder anymore, 'Are the Broncos a fluke?'"

Some would have called their takeaway tendency a fluke. But when it happened so often—and did again against the Steelers—it's better described as opportunism. The Broncos forced four turnovers— three interceptions off Terry Bradshaw and a fumble. John Schultz blocked a Steelers punt, setting the Broncos up at the Steelers 17-yard-line for a four-play drive that gave Denver an early 7-0 lead. The teams exchanged scores, but the Steelers never led.

The Steelers tried to intimidate the Broncos. Just before halftime, "Mean" Joe Greene punched starting offensive lineman Paul Howard, and then punched center Mike Montler one play later. A brawl nearly broke out.

But the Broncos opted to take care of business on the field, and what was finally the Steelers' undoing was Denver's continued takeaway touch. None were more massive than a pair of Tom Jackson interceptions in the final seven minutes of the game. Jackson returned them 32 and 17 yards, setting up a Jim Turner field goal and, finally, the 34-yard touchdown pass from Craig Morton to Jack Dolbin with 1:44 left that clinched the game. An earlier Jackson fumble recovery had set up a second-quarter touchdown, completing a game that was arguably the best in his career.

"I'm supposed to make the big plays happen as a weakside linebacker," Jackson said.

And by doing so, he pushed his team to legitimacy, once and for all.

"Hey, we're bona fide," said Thompson. "It's been a long time coming—too long. But we're there now."

PLAYING THROUGH PAIN

Craig Morton was closing in on the ultimate redemption: a chance to return to the Super Bowl, to become the first quarterback to start for two different teams in the game, and to do so against the team that benched him, since the Dallas Cowboys were expected to easily run through the NFC playoffs to Super Bowl XII—and did.

But that was a long way from his mind and the Broncos. His lingering hip injury—and the measures he was forced to take in order to play—was his focal point. Morton checked into a local hospital on Christmas, one day after beating the Steelers. He spent the week before the 1977 AFC Championship hospitalized, repeatedly having blood and fluid drained from the hip and thigh that had been bothering him for weeks.

The game plan was brought to Morton as he convalesced but backup Norris Weese ran the offense in practice. The sessions were closed to the media, so nothing leaked. Over the years, the NFL has become more stringent about how injuries must be reported. That hasn't kept some teams from circumventing the rules by listing dozens of players as "questionable," which is supposed to indicate a 50-50 chance of playing.

But questions about injury reports aren't a recent development, and after Morton played the entire AFC Championship game, questions were raised by the top of the NFL food chain: commissioner Pete Rozelle. He was peeved that the Broncos had kept the severity of Morton's condition a secret. "There should have been more candor. What the Broncos did was wrong," Rozelle said after the Broncos' win.

Miller said he only answered the questions in front of him.

"We didn't hide anything," he said at the time. "Nobody asked me if Craig had thrown a ball."

"M&M"

Since coming to Denver midway through the 1972 season, Haven Moses had been the Broncos' best deep threat since Lionel Taylor was catching everything in sight during the 1960s. But his numbers had declined after injuries forced Charley Johnson to the bench, and eventually to retirement.

Morton changed that. His willingness to stay in the pocket for as long as possible and take the hit as he threw gave Moses more chances to get open. He hit his statistical peak not in his mid-20s, but in his early 30s—after Morton arrived.

But it took a few months in 1977 for Moses to understand what Morton could do for his career.

"When they made the trade, it really didn't come out and hit me," Moses said in the 1977 postseason. "It wasn't like Denver got someone along the line of Bob Griese or Bert Jones."

But in 1977, Morton was the equal of those stellar passers of that era. And the AFC Championship against the Raiders displayed what they could accomplish together.

Morton keyed on Moses early; on two of the Broncos' first four plays, he looked for Moses downfield. Both fell incomplete, and the second pass, into traffic down the middle, was nearly intercepted by Oakland safety Jack Tatum.

The third time was the charm. Morton gingerly dropped back, turning for a play-action fake. From the Denver 19-yard-line, seven yards behind the line of scrimmage, he spotted Moses cutting toward the Raiders sideline at midfield, with two steps of separation from Oakland cornerback Skip Thomas, a defender who answered to the nickname "Dr. Death." Thomas caught up to Moses at the Oakland 40-yard-line, but tried to bring him down high, and Moses easily shook him off and sprinted the rest of the way.

Seventy-four yards, touchdown. The frigid, 18-degree day warmed up fast. Mile High went mad. Teammates mobbed Moses in the north end zone, but Morton was not among them; all he could do was hobble back to the Broncos' sideline to receive his congratulations.

The Broncos had been down 3-0 when Morton hit Moses. They never trailed again. Morton continued to key on Moses, and he caught four more passes for 96 yards, finishing the day with 168 yards on five receptions. M&M accounted for 20 more yards together than anyone else on the offense, and the Broncos held on for the 20-17 victory that sent them to Super Bowl XII.

The win was typical of the 1977 season; the Broncos forced three Oakland turnovers and held the Raiders to just 4.1 yards per play. But the explosion of Morton and Moses was something that couldn't have been foreseen in Week 1, when the passing game had no rhythm and the offense remained a work in progress.

The win was tinged with controversy; to this day, the Raiders maintain that Rob Lytle fumbled near the goal line in the third quarter, allowing Oakland's Mike McCoy to recover. Head linesman Ed Marion whistled the play dead, claiming Lytle's forward progress was stopped. Given the reprieve, the Broncos scored one play later when Jon Keyworth plunged over the goal line.

Said Miller: "All season long, they said we were too young and that we didn't belong here. I wonder if they believe we're for real now? I guarantee you we're for real."

In the emotional locker room, most Broncos whooped and hollered in jubilation, much like the fans who stormed the field. Morton celebrated quietly, not because of the pain, but the emotion of the moment. His circuitous road back to the Super Bowl was unlike any other to that point, and it would take another three decades before Kurt Warner traveled a similar path.

"It's not the hip," Morton told *Sports Illustrated* in the locker room after the win. "I'm frankly just overcome with emotion."

SUPER LETDOWN

For the two weeks that followed the AFC Championship, the Broncos' franchise history was revisited by writers and broadcasters from coast to coast. Despite their gradual rise to competitiveness in the previous four seasons, the Broncos were regarded as an out-of-nowhere Cinderella story. And although the defense defined the Broncos, the protagonist of Super Bowl XII was to be Morton, as he would stare down the team that jettisoned him in 1974 and Roger Staubach, the quarterback who beat him out for the starting job.

It was a dream scenario for Morton, and for anyone who believes in the power of redemption. It quickly became a nightmare, as Morton was pummeled by pass rushers.

Although the Orange Crush held its own and kept the Broncos within shouting distance, it was Dallas' "Doomsday Defense" that turned in its magnum opus and owned the day. For the first, and still only, time in Super Bowl history, the game's most valuable player award was shared, and it was split between two defenders: defensive tackle Randy White and defensive end Harvey Martin.

They earned it by rattling Morton and the Broncos' offense. He finished with as many interceptions (four) as completions. He was sacked twice in 17 pass plays. Finally, after narrowly missing a fifth interception with the Broncos down 20-3, Morton was pulled for Norris Weese, whose mobility allowed him to escape the pocket and temporarily took the edge off Dallas' pass rush.

Weese took advantage of good field position after a 67-yard Rick Upchurch kickoff return to lead the Broncos to a touchdown, but he, too, couldn't escape the Cowboys' pass rush. With 7:11 remaining, he was sacked by Martin and fumbled—the Broncos' eighth turnover. Dallas' Aaron Kyle recovered, and the Cowboys clinched the game one play later on a Robert Newhouse-to-Golden Richards touchdown pass.

The dream was over. But not the enthusiasm. Broncos fans had taken over the Louisiana Superdome, and as the game wound through its final moments, many fans chanted, "We love you!" to their team.

SHUFFLING QUARTERBACKS

Morton's struggles in Super Bowl XII and his ever-growing list of medical concerns had the Broncos thinking about the future in 1978. Morton was the starter but, by October, was injured. In a three-week stretch in October, the Broncos started three different quarterbacks. First, Morton gave way to Weese. Then it was back to Morton, and then on to Craig Penrose, a fourth-round pick in 1976 from San Diego State who had started the final two games of his rookie year before being benched for Morton in 1977.

Weese had the credibility from leading the Broncos' only touchdown drive in Super Bowl XII, but his scrambling style was never going to be ideal for the offense and would only expose him to injury. He was an energetic, if unrefined, quarterback, and the offense was inconsistent when he had the chance to run it.

Penrose got the star turn; he was at the controls for the first half of the Broncos' *Monday Night Football* game against the Chicago Bears on October 16. This game was his big chance, and he was effective enough, completing 7-of-11 passes for 74 yards … and then sustained a rib injury late in the second quarter that nagged him the rest of the season. Morton returned to close out the 16-7 win, and Penrose made just one more start in his Denver career.

Although Penrose had "the strongest arm among Denver quarterbacks," according to the Broncos' 1979 media guide, he only threw five passes that season and was part of a trade with the Jets for quarterback Matt Robinson the following year.

In 1978, the defense allowed Denver to overcome its instability under center to their second consecutive division title. But a playoff rematch with Pittsburgh was nothing like their Christmas Eve duel in 1977. No team had adapted better to the NFL's massive rules changes for the 1978 season than the Steelers, who used the restrictions on contact between defenders and receivers to unleash a deep passing game that complemented their still-potent power running attack of Franco Harris and Rocky Bleier. Two long touchdown passes in the fourth quarter turned a competitive game into a rout, and the Broncos fell, 33-10.

During that game, Miller replaced Morton with Weese, echoing the change made during Super Bowl XII eleven-and-a-half months earlier. After the Pittsburgh loss, Morton would lament, "I was just taken out and I don't know why."

When the 1979 regular season opened, the starter was Weese. For the second time in his career, Morton had been demoted in favor of a less experienced, but more mobile, quarterback. But Miller described the competition as "Two No. 1 quarterbacks and a very competent backup in Craig Penrose."

THE BRONCOS' GREATEST COMEBACK

Never was Morton's persistence better displayed than on September 23, 1979, when the 2-1 Broncos dug themselves a 34-10 third-quarter hole to the explosive Seahawks.

Morton started the game on the bench, just as he had the previous three weeks. The Broncos had averaged 14.3 points in those games, and Weese was inconsistent, but Morton, in a relief appearance in a Week 2 loss to the Los Angeles Rams, had also failed to move the team effectively.

But after Weese threw his second interception of the game, he was benched for Morton, who took over with 9:19 left in the third quarter. The impact was profound. Morton completed five consecutive passes for 77 yards, the last of which was to offensive lineman Dave Studdard, who scored on a tackle-eligible play. He followed that with two more touchdown passes in the next two minutes and thirty-four seconds, aided by a Bob Swenson interception and a three-and-out forced by the roused defense.

Three touchdowns in less than three minutes. Morton had completed eight of nine passes for 136 yards since coming into the game, and the deficit was down to three points. Morton lead another scoring drive the next time he saw the football, and the Broncos had the biggest comeback in franchise history, for a 37-34 win.

"When I sent Morton in, I just told him, 'Let's go; we're going to win,'" Miller said.

Weese returned to the starting lineup in the following two weeks, but the offense lumbered to just 10 points in those games. The Broncos split them, thanks to the defense pitching a shutout of the explosive San Diego Chargers; the 7-0 score was exactly the same as the last time Don Coryell had led a team into Mile High Stadium: the memorable season opener of 1977, when he led the St. Louis Cardinals. But Weese emerged from that game with a knee injury, and Morton made his first start of 1979 a week later. Weese never started again for the Broncos.

ELEVATED EXPECTATIONS

Broncos fans had to accustom themselves to a new perspective after Super Bowl XII. The scrappy-underdog days were gone—and they have yet to return. Their team had arrived. Inching above .500 and being competitive was no longer good enough. The playoff losses that concluded the 1978 and 1979 seasons didn't engender the same warm feelings that existed in the wake of the Super Bowl XII defeat. Indeed, these represented lost opportunities.

In 1977 and 1978, the Broncos had capitalized on a void at the top of the AFC West. The Raiders had peaked in their Super Bowl XI run of 1976, then had a slight, but steady fade, as John Madden retired, Ken Stabler aged, and stalwarts like Willie Brown and Fred Biletnikoff retired. The San Diego Chargers began rising in 1978 after replacing head coach Tommy Prothro with the innovative Coryell, but the "Air Coryell" offense didn't start soaring until 1979, and didn't reach cruising altitude until the following year. Kansas City had embarked on a second post-Hank Stram rebuilding phase under new coach Marv Levy and Seattle had a dazzling offense but a dreadful defense, and weren't a threat to win the division.

The 1979 campaign came down to the regular-season finale at San Diego: winner-take-all for the AFC West title. The game was played on Monday night, evidence of how far the Broncos had advanced in the 1970s, from national afterthought to a team expected to play significant games in December. Once again, the defense contained an explosive offense, holding the Chargers to 17 points and forcing five turnovers. But the Broncos did San Diego one better, with six giveaways, including four Morton interceptions—three of which came in the fourth quarter. Two were in the red zone. The Broncos lost 17-7 and settled for the consolation prize: a wild-card trip to Houston six days later.

In the Astrodome, Denver fell 13-7 in one of the most physical games in team history. The Broncos' defense knocked Houston's three key skill players—running back Earl Campbell, quarterback Dan Pastorini, and wide receiver Ken Burrough—out of the game, and none would play a week later. But the Broncos' offense collapsed. A 50-yard Fred Steinfort field-goal attempt slammed into an upright. Morton threw one touchdown, but tossed an interception and was sacked six times. A shouting match on the sideline among Miller, Reeves, and Weese ensued, the frustrations of a scattershot offensive season finally boiling over.

The Broncos had made three consecutive postseason appearances, but the returns had diminished each time. Opponents were starting to figure out how to find occasional holes in the Broncos' still-stellar defense. The running game was in transition. Morton was 36 and feeling the painful results of the hits he'd accumulated in his career.

As the Broncos flew home from Houston in the late-night hours of December 23, 1979, they had no way of knowing that the championship window for this generation had closed.

Chapter Three

The 1980s

Moments after the crushing wild-card loss in Houston, Red Miller set the tone for 1980, telling reporters, "We must analyze and do something about our offense next year. That's my first concern at this time."

The still-elite Orange Crush defense had just one limitation: it couldn't play more than half the possessions in a game. What Miller and general manager Fred Gehrke did to try and help it was bold, and well-intentioned, but didn't work.

In the off-season, Broncos sent first- and second-round draft picks and backup quarterback Craig Penrose to the New York Jets for quarterback Matt Robinson. Miller and the Broncos gambled that Robinson would be the quarterback of the near- and long-term future, and would end the shuffling between Weese and Morton that defined the frustrating 1979 season.

Robinson finally beat out Morton at the end of training camp. The collaboration started off well enough. In Robinson's second start—and first at Mile High Stadium—he ran for two touchdowns and led the Broncos to a 41-20 rout of Dallas, piling up more points on the Cowboys' famed Doomsday Defense than anyone had in a decade. The sun was shining—literally and figuratively—on the Broncos on that September afternoon. The gambit to mortgage the future on Robinson seemed set to pay massive dividends.

Then the Broncos lost their next two games, scoring 14 fewer points in them than they did against Dallas alone. The second of the defeats, a 23-14 loss at New England, was marred by the conduct of Schaefer Stadium fans, with scores of arrests of drunken, disorderly patrons and dozens of fights throughout the stands.

The New England crowd collectively lived up to the brewer's longtime slogan: "the one beer to have when you're having more than one." Meanwhile, the Broncos staggered and never quite recovered.

"We are not used to losing," Miller said.

Neither were Broncos fans, but they didn't react with the vitriol evident nine years earlier after Lou Saban settled for that infamous draw against Miami.

Robinson was yanked late in the second quarter of a Monday night game against Washington two weeks later, having thrown for just 43 yards on 5-of-11 passing with an interception. Denver went on to defeat Washington, 20-17, and Morton remained the starter.

But the 1980 Broncos kept stepping on the banana peels they avoided the previous years, making for one of the most difficult seasons in Broncos history. It didn't match the early years for hopelessness, but the 8-8 finish was the team's first non-winning season in five years and first out of the postseason in four.

Denver fans had quickly become accustomed to the playoffs, and their expectations and hopes soared after the Robinson trade. But by December, Robinson was effectively finished as a quarterback. He started the meaningless season finale, completing just nine of 23 passes. The following August, Robinson was waived. The only positive from the entire experience was that the picks the Broncos dealt to the Jets didn't amount to much. The first-rounder was dealt onward to San Francisco and used on defensive tackle Jim Stuckey, who played seven steady, unspectacular seasons. The second-rounder was used to take wide receiver Ralph Clayton, who never caught a regular-season pass.

Farewell to the Phipps Brothers—and Red, Too

The 1980 season was the final one for Gerry and Allan Phipps, who sold the team to Canadian investor Edgar Kaiser. Pro football was mushrooming into a massive business incomprehensible when the Phippses first got involved as minority investors in 1961.

But the ownership change was messy in terms of its fallout to the organization. Less than two weeks after the sale to Kaiser was finalized, Miller and Gehrke were fired. Gehrke had been with the Broncos in various capacities since 1965, and was involved in myriad aspects of the organization—even the décor of the office. An art major in college who designed the first helmet logo in NFL history (the ram horns), Gehrke took dozens of posters spotlighting each NFL team and created a mural from them on the wall of the lobby at Broncos headquarters. (Two decades after the Broncos left the Logan Street facility, it was still there.)

But it was the firing of Miller that shook the Broncos and their fans to the core. Both men were sacked on March 9—an unusual date, but one that came after meetings between them and Kaiser.

Miller remains the only head coach to have worked a Senior Bowl and been subsequently fired before the next season. He resurfaced a year later to coach the Denver Gold of the United States Football League in that circuit's first season, but was fired two and a half months into the spring campaign.

That dismissal was a relief, as Miller would later recall.

"We definitely had the lowest budget in the USFL," he told the *New York Times* in 1988. "On the road, we stayed at what might have been the original Holiday Inns. Once, in Michigan, the beds were so loose, you could barely sleep in them. We'd have to throw the mattresses on the floor just to get a night's sleep.

"In Philadelphia, we're getting on the hotel elevator and this lady's in there, all shaken up. Told us she'd just been robbed at gunpoint. We're thinking, 'Oh, great.'"

After the experience, exacerbated by slipshod ownership, Miller never coached again. He later worked as an investment broker, where he was as successful out of the gate as he was as Broncos head coach, earning a national sales award in his first year on the job. He flourished in the financial sector until he retired. But he always kept football in the corner of his eye. Two decades later, at the invitation of John Elway and John Fox, Miller could be seen in the VIP tent and near the sideline at Broncos training camp watching the new generation go about its work.

"They're bigger all over," Miller said. "We had big guys, but we didn't have as many big guys. We had fast guys, [but] not as many fast guys."

But in that era, the Broncos had enough to be a consistent contender, and although Miller's name is not in the team's Ring of Fame, his place of honor in Broncos lineage is assured. Other coaches have and will guide the Broncos to the Super Bowl, but Miller will always be the first.

ROPING IN REEVES

The relatively late date of Miller's firing and the hiring of Cowboys assistant coach Dan Reeves to replace him barely twenty-four hours later evoked memories of the circumstances around Miller's hire four years earlier.

"One of the toughest things for me when I came here was replacing Red. It wasn't a popular thing to do, taking his place. He was very popular with the people of Denver," Reeves would recall later in his Broncos tenure. "Besides, Denver people don't like Texans in general.

"And one night I went out and I had on my Super Bowl ring— the one I got with the Cowboys after we beat Denver (in Super Bowl XII). Some women saw it and said, 'You should know better than to wear that around here.' I never did again."

Of course, Reeves wasn't a Texan by birth or background; he was born and raised in Georgia, and matriculated at the University of South Carolina. His profound accent was Southern, not Texan. But he would always be connected with the Cowboys, the only professional team he had known before coming to Denver. He began his coaching career under Tom Landry in 1972, while he was still one of Dallas' running backs.

Reeves was Kaiser's only choice. The Cowboys were metronomic in their success, having just completed their fifteenth consecutive winning season. They drafted and developed better than anyone in the league, overcoming the chronically low draft position that came with their success with scouting philosophies that were ahead of their time and shrewd trades. One couldn't blame Kaiser, or any NFL team, for wanting to tap into a philosophy that was proven to work. A year later, George Halas and his Chicago Bears would mimic the Broncos, nabbing Mike Ditka off Landry's staff.

The youngest coach in the NFL didn't completely overhaul the coaching staff. Defensive coordinator Joe Collier remained in place;

Reeves would be the fifth head coach under whom he worked with the Broncos.

Reeves' age at the time—thirty-seven—worked in his favor.

"We needed a young organization and we need young men," said Kaiser.

1981: THE YOUNGEST COACH, AND THE OLDEST PLAYER

Reeves was eleven months younger than the quarterback he inherited, the one who had earned a reputation as a survivor—of both hits from defenders and attempts to replace him. One local headline called Morton "The Quarterback Who Won't Go Away."

Norris Weese, Craig Penrose, and Matt Robinson all had their chances. But one by one, they dropped the ball, and by 1981, everything finally came up Morton once again. With his old Cowboys teammate Reeves on the sideline as the NFL's youngest head coach at the time, Morton started from Week 1 onward and had the best statistical season of his career—and the best for any Broncos quarterback to that point. His 21 touchdown passes was a career high, as was his 90.8 rating. His yardage total of 3,195 was also the best of his career, and broke Frank Tripucka's twenty-one-year-old franchise record.

Reeves and Morton were close as Cowboys teammates—so close, in fact, that Reeves was in Morton's wedding party. But Morton didn't reclaim the job because of old-school sentiment that dated back to the Cowboys' Cotton Bowl years; he got it back because he could still sling the football, despite a laundry list of infirmities that left him immobile in the pocket.

"Give him time and he'll throw the eyes out of the bail," Reeves said during Morton's renaissance season. "His arm's as good as it ever was."

With Morton slinging passes and young Steve Watson setting a then-club record with 1,244 receiving yards, the Broncos finished with their fifth winning season in six years. Watson rang up his tally on just 60 catches—a 20.7-yard average that remains the highest for any Broncos receiver with at least 25 receptions in a single season. The 95-yard Morton-to-Watson touchdown strike against Detroit on October 11, 1981, remains the Broncos' longest play from scrimmage since 1962; a 93-yard connection by the same men two weeks earlier against the Chargers is the second-longest in the last half-century.

But in the regular-season finale that the Broncos needed to win in order to take the AFC West, Morton and the offense froze in the 14-degree chill of Chicago's Soldier Field. He threw a pair of interceptions that were returned for touchdowns, and was sacked five times. Steve DeBerg relieved him and threw a pair of second-half touchdown passes that narrowed an 18-point deficit, but the Broncos fell to the Bears, 35-24.

"The wind was blowing and it was just cold," defensive end Rulon Jones would later recall. "When it got cold, it was tough for him to move. We were sure we would win and go to the playoffs. Well we didn't win and it was probably the most uncomfortable game I have ever been in."

The next night, San Diego defeated Oakland, taking the AFC West away from the Broncos, who finished 10-6 but lost not only a tiebreaker for the division, but the last wild-card spot, which went to the Buffalo Bills.

A year later, Morton was demoted to the third team as Reeves sought to get more playing time for Steve DeBerg, acquired in a 1981 trade from the San Francisco 49ers. Morton was less than three months away from his fortieth birthday when he made his final career start, a 17-10 loss to the Seahawks on November 21, 1982.

"I think Dan made the decision based on what he wants to do over the long run," Morton said.

Morton was honored before his final home game and eventually inducted into the Ring of Fame. At the time of his last game, he defined jersey No. 7 in the orange and blue. That would change in the most resounding fashion possible months later.

STRIKING OUT

The 1982 season remains the biggest anomaly in NFL history. The players' strike tore the season asunder after two games and lasted eight weeks, lingering into November. An additional week of games was added to the regular season, creating a nine-game sprint to the playoffs that lent itself to odd results. Defending champion San Francisco slumped to a 3-6 finish. Miami won the AFC and made it to Super Bowl XVII with a young starting quarterback, David Woodley, who struggled so greatly in the title game that his replacement was drafted three months later. Green Bay and St. Louis made the postseason for the only time in the 1980s.

And the Broncos endured their only losing season for a twelve-year stretch. By winning percentage, their 2-7 finish remains the worst since the franchise moved out of the Quonset hut in 1967.

An early sign of the ambivalence some Broncos felt about the strike came in the opening week of the preseason. Throughout the league, entire teams met at midfield before games to shake hands, intending to show solidarity. The Broncos were the only team that did not want to do so.

"A few players got together and basically, it was, 'No,'" said Barney Chavous, the defensive lineman who was the Broncos' representative to the NFL Players' Association. A few other scattered players around the league also did not participate, but the Broncos were the sole group to do so en masse.

SQUARING UP AGAINST MORTALITY

Real life—and death—intrudes on football from time to time. The Broncos have dealt with their share of it in their fifty-four years, and a day after the 1982 season ended, they suffered a massive loss when defensive backfield coach Richie McCabe died of abdominal cancer, aged forty-eight.

McCabe became ill during that season's strike. In those days, it was common for men to fight an illness like this in private, with stoicism. McCabe wanted to share his struggle and his perspective with Broncos fans, so he submitted to an interview with the *Rocky Mountain News*, where he talked about coming to terms with his impending fate.

"When I was a kid back in Pittsburgh, I learned from the Baltimore Catechism the purpose of life: Know God, serve God, and seek eternity with Him forever. You know, that's a nice little paragraph," McCabe said.

"But does a first-grader understand that? Hell, no. Does a person forty years old understand that? Hell, no. But face death and you'll understand it.

"I've never questioned, 'Why me?' But I have asked, 'Lord, let me have one good night of rest,' or, 'Lord, let me be able to eat one good meal,' or, 'Lord, let me go into work for just one hour. It's amazing how important the details are; it's the small things I never considered before.

"I've asked the Lord to help me win a football game in the past, but I came to the conclusion He was too busy. But there were times when I needed help. Sitting here listening to records is fine in the daylight, but there's something about the night. It's fearful when you can't sleep. That can be really tough.

"I've got a battle and I won't tell you I don't ... they (doctors) won't promise me anything over ten years. But then the doctor asked me if I could assure him he'd be here in five years. Hell, for that matter, we're all the next plane ride away from death, aren't we?"

Two years and three months later, tight ends and special teams coach Fran Polsfoot would succumb to brain cancer at the age of fifty-seven. During his battle, he remained ever the coach, hoping to motivate patients going through the same struggle as he did. When Polsfoot went to the hospital in for chemotherapy treatments, he would hand out T-shirts that said, "Life's battles don't always go to the stronger or faster man. Sooner or later, the man who wins is the man who thinks he can."

The Elway Earthquake

Steve DeBerg had started five games in 1982 before giving way to Mark Herrmann in the season finale. But neither appeared to be the long-term answer, and the Broncos headed into 1983 facing a situation similar to ones they'd seen in previous decades when trying to replace starters who led the team for multiple years.

In 1983, the Broncos seemed poised for something different. The best quarterback class in recent memory stared at them, and the Broncos had the No. 4 overall pick, the highest for the team since the common draft between the AFL and NFL was instituted in 1967. But with that pick, and only John Elway off the board among quarterbacks, the Broncos opted for a franchise left tackle, taking Northwestern's Chris Hinton.

At the moment of the pick, it seemed to indicate a vote of confidence in DeBerg and Mark Herrmann, the two quarterbacks left standing after Craig Morton's retirement. Hinton was flown to Denver, introduced to media and was even greeted by autograph seekers upon landing at Stapleton Airport. It was an altogether new experience for Hinton, who had endured a thirty-four-game losing streak in college.

But behind the scenes, the wheels turned. The Baltimore Colts had selected Elway with the No. 1 overall pick, and he had reiterated his desire to not play there and exercise his option to play baseball with the New York Yankees, who picked him in the first round of the 1979 Major League Baseball draft.

The baseball threat was a serious one. Elway had already had a stellar season for the Oneonta (New York) Yankees in the short-season A-level New York-Penn League, batting .318 with a .896 OPS in 1982. He was patient at the plate, took his share of walks, could hit for power, and had speed to spare. It was reasonable to expect that if Elway had played baseball, he would have been in the major leagues by 1985 and could have been primed for a lengthy, stellar career.

But it's likely he never would have been the transformative star he could be in football.

"If nothing happened within a week, I was going to sign with the Yankees," Elway said just after his situation had been settled. "It's not that I thought, 'God, not the Yankees,' but my preference was to play professional football."

And that knowledge kept teams calling the Colts. The negotiations became serious between them and the Broncos but were not conducted by the general managers or coaches. Instead, Broncos owner Edgar Kaiser dealt with Colts owner Robert Irsay, an impetuous owner who had habitually threatened to move his team. After one 1976 preseason game, Irsay stormed into the locker room and excoriated his team, causing his coach, Ted Marchibroda, to quit in protest, just nine months after leading the Colts to a division title. Only a threatened walkout by the team was able to convince all parties to reconcile. But the threat of Irsay going Vesuvius never ebbed.

Colts general manager Ernie Accorsi was willing to wait for what he felt was a fair deal for a franchise quarterback. Irsay didn't. He agreed to send Elway to Denver in exchange for Hinton, Herrmann, and the Broncos' first-round pick in the 1984 NFL Draft.

The news broke during the evening of May 2, 1983. A short pass away from Mile High Stadium sat McNichols Sports Arena, where the Denver Nuggets were trying to salvage Game 4 of their conference semifinal series with the San Antonio Spurs after falling behind three games to none. As the Nuggets took a 22-point halftime lead, the biggest trade in Broncos history was made; Elway signed his contract. Reeves, who had been sitting courtside, dashed for the exit.

At that point, the media caught on and word spread. Press row became a ghost town. Television reporters, radio commentators, and newspaper columnists grabbed their notes and gear, shoved it in briefcases and dashed to the press conference. It was held at 10:30 p.m.— barely on time to make the next day's morning papers in Denver and too late to beat the deadlines in the Eastern and Central time zones.

But there was no use in holding back. If Elway had been unveiled to Denver media at 3:30 a.m., the room would have still been packed and television stations would have gone back on the air—this was 1983, remember, and many still signed off for the night—to cover it.

Kaiser had altered the destiny of the franchise forever. No one knew that more than Reeves, who saw first-hand in Dallas with Roger Staubach how an athletic, multi-dimensional quarterback could galvanize the offense—and the entire team.

"This is the closest I've ever been to heaven," Reeves said as Elway was introduced. "It's my job now not to mess up."

There were, of course, complications. Long-time Broncos antagonist Al Davis alleged that the NFL had blocked the attempts of his Los Angeles Raiders to trade for Elway. Hinton, who was initially upset by the deal, suggested through his lawyer that he would reconsider an earlier contract offer from the Chicago Blitz of the upstart USFL, but ultimately warmed to being a Colt and became one of their most beloved players in that era.

And Elway was not guaranteed anything regarding his role for the 1983 season. As the trade was announced, Reeves maintained that DeBerg was still the No. 1 quarterback and Elway would have to beat him out. DeBerg had experienced this before, in 1979 when San Francisco drafted Joe Montana. He would experience it again in 1985 and 1987, when the Buccaneers replaced him with Steve Young and then Vinny Testaverde.

When Week 1 arrived on September 4, Elway was the starter. Although DeBerg would start six games in 1983, it would not be until he got to Kansas City in 1988 before he became a starting quarterback without the threat of a young passer who had a plausible chance to take his spot. By the time that happened, Elway had already taken the Broncos to a pair of Super Bowls and won a league MVP trophy.

WHAT DID ELWAY HAVE FOR LUNCH?

Until 1983, the Broncos' best quarterbacks were hand-me-downs— from the CFL (Frank Tripucka), Houston Oilers (Charley Johnson), and the New York Giants (Craig Morton). Elway was different: a freshly-minted athletic wonder who was considered the best quarterback prospect in a generation.

The closest thing to Elway that the city of Denver had prior to his arrival was David "Skywalker" Thompson with the ABA and NBA Nuggets, the dunking, slashing maestro who by his fourth season was the highest-paid player in NBA history. (Thompson's career was subsequently derailed because of injuries and substance-abuse issues.) But when the Broncos had a star, it was different. The Nuggets mattered on the Denver sports scene, but the Broncos were the obsession.

And never had Denver been more obsessed over a player than Elway.

During his first training camp and preseason, he dominated the news. It was common to see at least five stories tied to Elway in the local papers each day. The "Elway Watch" chronicled his meals, his performance in practice, and even his thoughts on movies and predictions for the upcoming college football season.

"Too much Elway" was an unfathomable notion. Every step, every bite, every move Elway made could merit a banner headline or placement atop the five and six o'clock newscasts. While the intensity of this would soften as the months and years passed, the Colorado appetite for all things Elway has yet to ebb. Perhaps that helps explain the success of Elway's steakhouses, which now include a location at Denver International Airport to give passengers changing planes at the major hub a chance to sample a flavor of what has become a Denver institution.

STARING DOWN THE COLTS

Three months after the trade, the Colts filed a grievance with the league, claiming the Broncos committed a "breach of faith" in announcing the trade too soon and wanting the Broncos' second-round draft pick in 1984 as compensation for their trouble. The Colts claimed that they were wronged because the swap was announced before Hermann and Hinton were contacted. The NFL rebuffed the Colts' request.

Less than a month later, the Colts hosted the Broncos in Week 2. The teams were paired for a home-and-home in 1983 in a quirk of the scheduling formula that existed from 1978-94, in which the last-place finishers in the two divisions in each conference that had five teams played each other twice the following season.

Colts attendance had been faltering for a few years and cratered in 1981 and 1982, seasons in which the Colts went 2-22-1. But Elway's arrival galvanized Marylanders, 52,613 of whom crammed Memorial Stadium. The weather was brutally hot—99 degrees at kickoff—but emotions ran hotter. One sign hanging from the upper deck at Memorial Stadium simply read, "Kill Elway."

"I thought I'd get booed at first, but not for the whole first half," Elway said. "It can't get much worse than that."

For a second consecutive game, Elway struggled. He had been inconsistent in the Week 1 game at Pittsburgh and against Baltimore was sacked three times while completing nine of 21 passes. He was relieved late in the third quarter, came back in for three plays in the fourth quarter, was sacked a third time and then pulled for good in favor of DeBerg, who led the Broncos on two scoring drives to overturn a 10-3 deficit into a 17-10 win.

"I made the change strictly because we couldn't get the plays off," Reeves said. Elway was forced to take three delay-of-game penalties because of the din. "The crowd was very involved and every time we didn't get one (snap) off, they got more fired up.

"I've never heard anything like that. It was unreal."

The struggles for Elway continued in the following weeks until he was benched on October 5 in favor of DeBerg. The Broncos' offense ranked dead last in the league in yardage and Elway's quarterback rating at the time was 40.3.

But all that did was set up Elway's first comeback. First, he regained the starting job in November. Then, in Week 15 against Baltimore, he led the Broncos back from a 19-0 fourth-quarter deficit, flinging three touchdown passes in a 21-19 win.

After Elway's skittish September, the Broncos were starting to believe in their young quarterback.

"John Elway can put points on the board faster than I can add them up," linebacker Tom Jackson said.

The game-winning touchdown came on a fourth-and-2 from the Baltimore 26-yard-line with 44 seconds left. On the play, Elway found running back Gerald Willhite open. But Willhite was only in the clear because he had failed to pick up a blitzing Colts safety and taken off on his route.

"The safety was barreling down on me and Gerald was wide open. I just put it up there and prayed," Elway said.

The entire scenario looked familiar to Reeves, given his background with the Dallas Cowboys.

"I've seen this before. Roger Staubach got his reputation that way with great comebacks, and Danny White did it after him," Reeves said. "Now, our team is never really out of a game. They know they can always come back."

And they would know it for the next fifteen years.

With the win, the Broncos clinched their first playoff berth since 1979—and the games against Baltimore were the difference. Denver finished 9-7, while the Colts limped home 7-9 and missed out for the sixth consecutive season; by March, Irsay had agreed to move the team to Indianapolis. The moving vans dashed away from the Colts' Owings Mills, Maryland, headquarters in the middle of the night. A year later, Kush was fired.

Elway's reluctance to play for the Colts was justified. They would cycle through five coaches in the eight seasons after moving to Indianapolis. They didn't achieve stability until 1992, when they righted a past wrong by bringing back Ted Marchibroda thirteen years after firing him. By that time, Elway was thirty-two and had been to the Super Bowl three times.

As Elway Era Dawns, Gradishar Departs

Elway's first season was Randy Gradishar's last. After ten seasons, the linebacker retired, choosing not to linger on the field, although he remained with the organization for the next few years as the president of the club's youth foundation. He went out playing at an elite level; his final game was the Pro Bowl—his seventh—on January 29, 1984.

Three decades later, the Pro Football Hall of Fame has yet to call his name, even though a comparable contemporary, Giants inside linebacker Harry Carson, was welcomed into the fold in 2006. Thus, the Broncos' Orange Crush defense of the 1970s, which became one of the truly iconic defenses in league annals, remains unrepresented.

After he failed to make the Hall in 2008 as a finalist, his name passed through to the Seniors Committee.

"I call it the dead-man category," Gradishar deadpanned.

Teammate Floyd Little was inducted in 2010 through that avenue but Gradishar is realistic about the possibilities. The Seniors Committee can only nominate two potential inductees per year.

"It's a hard decision. You've got a jillion names, especially when you go in the dead category, and then you're dealing with a bunch. I don't know how they decide who comes up next year, to be honest."

Gradishar leans on his personal religious faith and tries not to worry. He turned 65 in 2017, moves better than he has in years thanks to a pair of knee replacements, and has maintained his ties with the team. In June 2013, he spoke to the current Broncos about leadership and positive visualization. He told them, "Picture yourself as the hero," something he was often during his ten seasons in orange and blue.

There are two cases that critics made against Gradishar's Hall candidacy. Both are easily refuted. The first is his ten-year career span, which some consider too brief.

"Gale Sayers played (seven seasons). Dick Butkus played nine. Did you ask them?" he said. "Some of those things that I've heard back are just ridiculous. It's like saying, 'Who's representing who?' It's like the committee is telling you—well, they don't believe you had 2,000 tackles."

And the perceived inaccuracy of that total—generally accepted to be 2,049—is the other case often made to scuttle Gradishar's candidacy. Tackles have never been an official statistic and in those days were kept by coaching staffs, leading to the perception that his totals were padded. But that issue doesn't seem to arise for other defensive players of that era the way it does for Gradishar.

"All these excuses came up," Gradishar said, "and it's like, 'Well, you're telling me you don't believe the tackles, so you're telling me that Joe Collier lied and the defensive staff lied?'

"People ask me and I say, 'Well, you can still go in when you're dead, so I have hope.' It'd be a great honor if that happens. Right now, being able to represent the Broncos and Colorado, and still being out here, it would just mean a lot."

BRONCOS AND RAIDERS: MUTUAL LOATHING

The Broncos-Raiders series wasn't really any kind of rivalry until 1977. To be rivals implies something mutual; prior to the Broncos' first playoff appearance, the Raiders barely gave Denver a second thought.

By 1984, that had changed. Although the Raiders had won a pair of Super Bowls in the previous four seasons while the Broncos had missed the playoffs three times, the ledger since the Broncos' breakthrough had read Raiders 8, Broncos 7. From 1983 through 1987, they were the only teams to win the AFC West. Even though the Raiders had moved to Los Angeles, the rivalry was reaching its boiling point.

On September 30, 1984, the heat between the clubs hit 212 degrees. Lyle Alzado—by then a Raider—fought with Broncos tight end Clarence Kay, who later found himself in a tussle with Raiders linebacker Rod Martin. Other scrums percolated after plays.

Finally, in the third quarter, tensions bubbled over. With the Broncos in goal-to-go and Elway scrambling toward the end zone, offensive tackle Ken Lanier and Raiders defensive lineman Sean Jones got into a no-rules, no-holds-barred brawl, the kind with which the Raiders were familiar from years of playing a physical, hold-nothing-back style. Jones ripped Lanier's helmet from his head. But it was Lanier who was ejected by referee Jerry Markbreit.

"The fight is my fault—for losing my cool," Jones admitted to *Sports Illustrated*. "But this stuff is getting ridiculous. Guys are holding us, tugging on us, and the officials aren't calling the fouls."

"A typical Raider-Bronco game," opined linebacker Tom Jackson, who by this point had seen twenty-three of them.

The Broncos had figured out how to counter the Raiders at their own game. As the 1980s progressed, they would get even better; in 1986-87, the Broncos ripped off their first four-game winning streak in the series, a feat they would not repeat again until 1995-96.

THE UNLIKELIEST GREAT SEASON

Statistical wonks might look back at the 1984 Broncos and be struck dumb. How could a team that boasted the No. 22 offense and No. 25 defense possibly finish with a winning record, let alone win more regular-season games than all but one team in Broncos history?

Takeaways.

As the Orange Crush began to blossom in 1976, forcing turnovers had always been a focal point. Sometimes the Broncos would get gashed for yardage, but with explosive defensive plays, they could compensate. Never was this more the case than in 1984, when the Broncos recovered 24 fumbles and intercepted 31 passes which matches the 1978 total for the Broncos' best since the AFL-NFL merger. Eight of those takeaways were returned for touchdowns, the most in Broncos history.

Time and attrition had taken its toll on the Orange Crush of the 1970s, but by 1984, new stars like defensive end Rulon Jones, safety Dennis Smith, and linebacker Karl Mecklenburg had emerged and blossomed. When all of them arrived, they had a crash course in Collier's defense: intricate, complex, and flexible enough to adapt to almost any attack.

"You could never work any harder than Joe. He did absolutely everything that he could to be prepared," Jones recalled in 2006. "He adapted to the players that he had. He wasn't a type of guy that was totally set on what he did. He adapted to things as he saw the need per game.

"There was a lot more of the mental part of the game with Joe Collier as defensive coordinator because we did so many different things. A lot of teams maybe had ten different defenses, where we may have had sixty or one hundred or something like that. We had quite a playbook to draw from.

"Joe had a great influence on what I did obviously because I was one of his players and he took into account my abilities and every ones on the team. He was a very unique guy as far as that goes and a great coach."

The 1984 season was a significant campaign for Jones, who had 11 sacks, the best total since his rookie season of 1980, when he amassed 11.5. Jones was hitting the prime of his career, and from 1984 to 1986, he had 34.5 sacks, played in two Pro Bowls, and was a first-team All-Pro once.

With Jones creating havoc from his defensive end spot, Denver sealed its first AFC West crown in six years with a 31-14 romp at Seattle in the regular-season finale. As with the game at San Diego to close the 1979 season, this was winner-takes-all in Week 16 for the AFC West crown, but this time, the Broncos rolled. The game featured the eighth defensive return touchdown of the year when Steve Foley sprinted 40 yards for a third-quarter touchdown that put the Broncos up 24-7.

But the magnum opus of this opportunistic defense—and the one game from this season that everyone would remember—came all the way back in Week 7.

THE SNOW BOWL

Being from icy Green Bay, Wisconsin, the Packers are used to playing in a little snow. But not as early as October 15, and not to the extreme they faced when they walked into Mile High Stadium and into an ambush of snowflakes and orange jerseys.

It was these conditions—well, the snow, at least—that spurred Dan Reeves' decision to take the wind and kickoff if the Broncos won the coin toss. It was one of the wisest decisions he ever made. On the first play from scrimmage, Packers running back Gerry Ellis lost his grip on the football and Steve Foley picked it up and scampered into the end zone with a 22-yard touchdown. After the kickoff, it was a near-instant-replay: fullback Jessie Clark picked up five yards and then fumbled, allowing Louis Wright to recover and sprint 27 yards for the score.

The Broncos became the first—and only—team to score two defensive touchdowns on the first two plays from scrimmage. Just 37 seconds had elapsed and the Broncos led, 14-0.

The 62,546 who had made it to Mile High Stadium were manic. Eventually the Packers settled down and adjusted and their offense found its footing. Green Bay outgained Denver 423 yards to 193, had 25 first downs to Denver's 10, and averaged 6.2 yards per play to the Broncos' 3.8. The reason for this was simple: as long as you don't have gale-force winds, snowy conditions often favor the offense, particularly one that passes, because cornerbacks can't quickly change direction and adapt to routes. The Packers had one of the game's most explosive passing offenses at the time, and they shredded the Broncos play after play.

"Everybody was tip-toeing around and sliding off their feet," Foley told *The Denver Post* in 2000.

But the Broncos didn't lose their turnover touch. They would intercept Packers quarterback Lynn Dickey once, while also recovering two more fumbles. Green Bay kicker Eddie Garcia missed a pair of field-goal attempts. The Packers had a minus-four turnover margin. In many ways, this was the game that encapsulated the entire year, and punctuated a season filled with magic.

And because this was on *Monday Night Football*, a nation just starting to enjoy autumn saw the wintry scenes and were mesmerized. The next day, calls buried Colorado ski resorts from vacationers making reservations for winter ski holidays.

ONE AND DONE, AGAIN

But the pixie dust finally ran out on December 30, when the 9-7 Steelers stormed into Mile High Stadium and handed the Broncos their first-ever home playoff loss, 24-17. The defense had done its part to prevent this, recovering a pair of first-quarter fumbles by Steelers quarterback Mark Malone in Pittsburgh territory. But only one of those takeaways resulted in points: an Elway touchdown pass that capped a five-play, 22-yard drive. The other fumble had led to a missed Rich Karlis field goal. This gave Pittsburgh the window to stay within shouting distance, setting up its subsequent comeback.

Meanwhile, Elway's first postseason start was a shaky one. He threw two touchdown passes, but also tossed a pair of interceptions, the costliest of these coming with 2:45 remaining, when safety Eric Williams stepped in front of an Elway pass and returned it to the Denver 2-yard-line. Running back Frank Pollard barged over the goal line three plays later, completing the Steelers' comeback from a 17-10 third-quarter deficit.

The loss was painful, and was the Broncos' fifth consecutive playoff defeat dating back to Super Bowl XII. But it did not tarnish the season. Elway showed glimpses of greatness throughout the year and the defense was a perfect complement. Reeves had won 60 percent of his games since taking the head-coaching job and was establishing himself as one of the brighter stars of a new coaching generation that included Joe Gibbs, Bill Parcells, and fellow ex-Dallas staffer Mike Ditka. But the Broncos couldn't count on eight defensive touchdowns every year. The offense would have to improve with Elway at the controls for the Broncos to remain a title threat.

PAT BOWLEN: A NEW MAN IN THE BIG CHAIR

The 1984 season was also significant because it was the first one under the stewardship of forty-year-old Pat Bowlen, who bought a majority, 60.8 percent stake in the team from Edgar Kaiser on March 23. Bowlen would buy the rest of the team a year later.

The impact of Bowlen's arrival was apparent. Players who needed to be re-signed were re-signed, most notably safety Dennis Smith, a four-year veteran who was only beginning to build a Ring of Fame-worthy résumé. He invested in improvements to the team's seventeen-year old Logan Street headquarters.

"I think one difference (between Kaiser and Bowlen) is that Pat has a driving obsession to win," Jackson said during Bowlen's first season in charge. "If organizations are built from the top down, then Pat is probably the perfect owner for us."

Added Elway: "There's no question he wants to win. The acquisitions he's made, his willingness to pay players to keep them here. Winning is the most important thing to him."

Winning meant treating his players right, a philosophy he wasted little time instituting in the franchise. An elite athlete himself—he is a lifelong runner who has completed marathons and the Ironman triathlon—he understood what would satisfy his players and put them in position to succeed.

"Basically, they want to be treated like human beings, not like chattels or pieces of equipment," Bowlen said in his first year with the Broncos. "That's as much a part of it as the money they're getting paid."

Bowlen had been involved in sports before. His business interests covered oil, real estate, and construction in Alberta. His construction business helped build Northlands Coliseum, which under different corporate names remains the home of the NHL's Edmonton Oilers to this day. He provided funding to the Canadian Football League's Montreal Alouettes.

He investigated an investment for a start-up team in the upstart USFL but decided against it, later telling the *Montreal Gazette*, "It is perhaps the worst investment you could ever make in professional sport." That the USFL went belly-up less than four years after its first kickoff shows how and why Bowlen accumulated the wealth to buy an NFL team: like a cool, successful blackjack player, Bowlen possessed the intelligence, savvy, and shrewdness in knowing when to hit and when to stay.

But the Broncos were different. Bowlen plunged into the business. He relocated from Edmonton to Denver. He was involved in the everyday administration of the organization until stepping back nearly three decades later.

When asked during his first season how long he planned to run the Broncos, Bowlen said, "Forever."

Thirty-three years, three world championships, eight conference championships, and eighteen playoff appearances later, his ledger as owner ranks among the best the game has ever known. His involvement with the owners' broadcast committee helped the league expand its television reach and revenues to stratospheric levels, making the NFL the envy of sports leagues worldwide. At some point in the future, there could be momentum for his enshrinement into the Pro Football Hall of Fame; for now, the Broncos' success will be his legacy.

THE FLYING SNOWBALL

For decades, Denver's fans have been among the NFL's best; passionate, raucous, and enthusiastic, while usually not crossing the line into boorishness or foul play. But November 11, 1985, remains the exception, and was the difference in granting the Broncos an ill-gotten, 17-16 *Monday Night Football* triumph over the San Francisco 49ers.

As 49ers placekicker Ray Wersching was about to attempt a 19-yard gimme field-goal attempt, a snowball landed in front of holder Matt Cavanaugh, disrupting the spot. Cavanaugh bobbled the football, picked it up and lobbed an incomplete pass into the end zone.

"There is no place for that kind of activity in pro football," said Dan Reeves. "I hope we don't ever see that again."

Nearly three decades later, the Broncos haven't.

Frank Tripucka was already a grizzled veteran—and had even been a head coach for a brief period in the Canadian Football League—by the time he lined up for the Broncos. *(Denver Broncos archives)*

Good seats were available at Bears Stadium in the first years of the franchise, as was the case for this game against the Houston Oilers, an early AFL power. The vertically striped socks are on full display. *(Denver Broncos archives)*

The wide-open American Football League was ahead of its time, and the balletic, one-handed catches of Lionel Taylor were worth more than the price of admission, even as the overall team struggled. *(Denver Broncos archives)*

The first save-the-team drive led to this sight: a filled Bears Stadium in 1965. Attendance shot up, even as the win totals stayed the same.
(Denver Broncos archives)

Cookie Gilchrist never did anything quietly, and even his publicity photograph— something close to the Heisman pose —was audacious. *(Denver Broncos archives)*

Game officials were frequently the target of Lou Saban's frustration during his years on Denver's sideline. *(Denver Broncos archives)*

For one season, Marlin "The Magician" Briscoe electrified the offense, and helped begin blazing a trail for African-American quarterbacks who followed him in the decades to come. *(Denver Broncos archives)*

The South Stands of Mile High Stadium was where fan passion boiled over, and left the finely attired Hank Stram and his Kansas City Chiefs running for cover—which, ironically, was in the locker room housed on the ground floor of the very stands where the craziest Bronco fans congregated. *(Denver Broncos archives)*

With Miami's Manny Fernandez in pursuit, Floyd Little prepares to sweep to the right in the 1971 season opener that would end in a tie, fan anger and, eventually, half-loaves of bread brandished in the South Stands. *(Denver Broncos archives)*

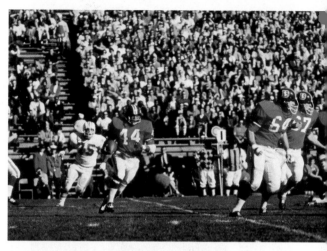

The 1974 coaching staff. In the front row, defensive coordinator Joe Collier, head coach John Ralston, and offensive coordinator Max Coley. In the back row, defensive backs coach Bob Gambold, wide receivers coach Kay Dalton, defensive line coach Doc Urich, linebackers coach Myrel Moore, and offensive line coach Jerry Frei. Frei would return to the Broncos in subsequent decades, first on Dan Reeves' staff, then in the 1990s as the director of college scouting. Collier would remain as defensive coordinator until 1988. Note how the Mile High Stadium upper decks stop behind them; the north end zone and east stands had yet to be expanded. *(Denver Broncos archives)*

A common sight in the 1970s: wide receiver Haven Moses, out in front of the defense, headed for the end zone. *(Denver Broncos archives)*

Owner Gerald Phipps was universally respected in the Broncos organization by coaches and players like Otis Armstrong. By the mid-1970s Phipps was no longer worried about saving the Broncos for Denver; he wanted a team that could contend for the Super Bowl. *(Denver Broncos archives)*

Red Miller was one of the final pieces of the Super Bowl puzzle. He brought a more personal touch to the head coaching position upon his hire in 1977, which he showed with defensive back Billy Thompson after a win at Kansas City. *(Denver Broncos archives)*

There was no question the 1977 Broncos were for real after a 27–13 win over Baltimore in a duel of 9-1 teams, and the fans wanted to proclaim the news as boldly as possible. *(Denver Broncos archives)*

Few sights stoked more fear in opposing quarterbacks in the Orange Crush era than Randy Gradishar. Hall of Famer Dan Fouts doesn't have good memories; he threw twice as many interceptions (28) as touchdown passes (14) in games against Gradishar-led defenses. *(Denver Broncos archives)*

Craig Morton bids farewell to Mile High Stadium before his final home game on December 19, 1982. When Morton arrived via trade in 1977, he was battered and considered by some to be washed up. He left as a franchise hero, destined for the Ring of Fame. *(Denver Broncos archives)*

Dan Reeves had plenty of points to make to John Elway during the quarterback's up-and-down rookie season of 1983. *(Denver Broncos archives)*

No Bronco looked less comfortable in a snowstorm than the barefoot Rich Karlis. But he was unfazed by the famous *Monday Night Football* snowstorm against Green Bay in 1984. His 30-yard field goal provided the decisive points in a 17-14 win. *(Denver Broncos archives)*

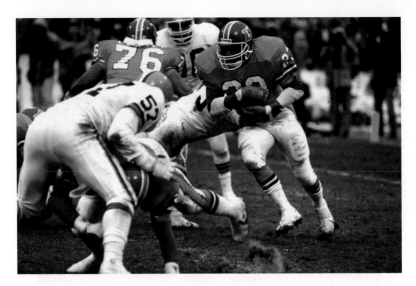

A tough, versatile running back, Sammy Winder helped kick-start "The Drive" in the 1986 AFC Championship Game by pulling the Broncos out from the shadow of their uprights. *(Denver Broncos archives)*

A 39-20 Super Bowl XXI loss to the New York Giants did not dampen local enthusiasm, as fans turned out for a parade saluting the team. Showing how times would become more cynical, the Broncos team that lost Super Bowl XLVIII would not receive a similar welcome home. *(Denver Broncos archives)*

Dan Reeves made the tough call to dismiss longtime defensive coordinator Joe Collier after the 1988 season. But Collier's replacement, Wade Phillips, energized the defense and helped the Broncos return to the Super Bowl. *(Denver Broncos archives)*

In his two seasons as Broncos head coach, Wade Phillips brought a mellow, calming presence—and hired Jim Fassel as offensive coordinator, which launched John Elway toward some of his most brilliant seasons. *(Denver Broncos archives)*

Mike Shanahan's return as head coach in 1995 helped propel the franchise to new heights. The three years he spent as San Francisco's offensive coordinator broadened his tactical perspective, and for four seasons together, he and Elway orchestrated the most powerful offense of its time. *(Denver Broncos archives)*

By 1998, Pat Bowlen had owned the Broncos for fourteen years and sat at the top of his sport. His team was on its way to its second consecutive world championship, and was planning for its move to a new stadium. *(Denver Broncos archives)*

John Elway salutes the Mile High Stadium fans as the 1998 AFC Championship trophy is awarded following a 23-10 win over the New York Jets. Two weeks later, Elway earned Super Bowl Most Valuable Player honors in a 34-19 win over the Falcons, his final game. *(Denver Broncos archives)*

One of the biggest trades in Broncos history brought them Champ Bailey, who spent 10 seasons shutting down one receiver after another and building a sure-fire Hall of Fame resume. *(Author archives)*

Jay Cutler became a Pro Bowler by his third season and looked poised to become the Broncos' franchise quarterback, but the firing of Mike Shanahan changed everything. *(Author archives)*

Tim Tebow was going to be Josh McDaniels' great project, but on-field struggles and off-field chaos led to McDaniels' dismissal before Tebow even made an NFL start. *(Author archives)*

Chris Kuper's attempt at playing cricket was a rare light moment in an otherwise disastrous team trip to London in 2010 that represents the franchise's modern nadir. *(Author archives)*

John Elway's first hire after being named executive vice president in 2011 was head coach John Fox. The two immediately set out putting together the pieces of a team shattered by five years of diminishing returns. *(Author archives)*

Tebow's unorthodox throwing motion and scattershot accuracy forced offensive coordinator Mike McCoy to change the offense on the fly in 2011. The college-style zone-read option he utilized minimized Tebow's weaknesses, played to his improvisational strengths, and helped the Broncos win their first division title in six years. *(Author archives)*

The Broncos gambled that Peyton Manning would be able to regain his arm strength and accuracy when they signed him in 2012. The move paid off, as Manning led the Broncos to to two Super Bowl appearances in his four seasons with the team, including a victory in Super Bowl 50, his final NFL game. *(Author archives)*

"MILE HIGH MAGIC"

Every so often, the Broncos win a home game in inexplicable fashion. In 2006, a 24-23 win over the Cincinnati Bengals on Christmas Eve was made possible when Brad St. Louis sailed an extra-point snap wide of holder Kyle Larson with forty-one seconds remaining.

But six days after the snowball game, it took two tries at blocking Bob Thomas' game-winning 40-yard field goal attempt in overtime to defeat the Chargers. On the first, safety Dennis Smith deflected Thomas' attempt, but the Broncos had called timeout before the snap, nullifying the play. Few in Mile High Stadium had heard referee Fred Silva blow the whistle over the din.

Remarkably, Smith blocked the re-kick, sprinting into the backfield from Thomas' left flank. The ball bounced back to the Denver 40-yard-line, where cornerback Louis Wright grabbed the football on the bounce and in stride. The holder, punter Ralf Mojsiejenko, was the only Charger with a chance, but he didn't really have one, anyway. Wright sprinted untouched to the north end zone with the game-winning touchdown.

"I didn't start smiling until I hit the end zone, because I know it's never over 'til it's over," Wright said.

Smith, however, was certain.

"When Louis picked the ball up, I put my hands in the air," he said. "I knew he was gone."

Wright jumped to the fence separating the stands from the field and was mobbed by fans on one side and teammates on the other. But wins like that would not be enough to return the Broncos to the playoffs.

GOOD, BUT NOT GOOD ENOUGH

To this day, the 1985 Broncos stand as the best team, by record, to miss the playoffs, although they would be eventually joined by the 2008 New England Patriots. Both teams finished 11-5, but lost tiebreakers for the playoffs. In both cases, other teams won divisions with 8-8 records.

In 1985, it was the Browns who took advantage of a weak AFC Central to make the postseason while the superior Broncos stayed home, consigned to watching the 11-5 Jets and Patriots duel in the wild-card round—and then watching the Browns face the Dolphins in the divisional playoffs.

"It just doesn't feel fair that you could be 11-5 and two weeks from now be watching a team that's 8-8 play in the playoffs," said linebacker Tom Jackson.

The Broncos lost out because of a point-differential tiebreaker that had a higher priority at the time than today; the Jets and Patriots were at plus-129 and plus-72, respectively, while the Broncos were at plus-51, with six wins coming by a touchdown or less.

The Broncos had won a rare Friday night season finale at Seattle to finish with eleven wins, then came home to watch the Sunday games. Powerless to control their future, they saw the Patriots beat the Bengals and the Jets take out the Browns.

"It really feels unfair. I just don't know any other way to put it," said Jackson.

The Broncos would eventually make two Super Bowls with that same 11-5 regular-season finish. In 1985, it was good for nothing but a lump of coal in their holiday stocking. Shortly after the season, Cowboys general manager Tex Schramm, the chairman of the league's Competition Committee, announced there would be no changes in the postseason format just because the Broncos had been victimized by it.

"If you happen to lose out in the tiebreaker, that's the way it is," said an unapologetic Schramm. His own team was one game worse than the Broncos, but made the postseason, finishing 10-6.

WHEN ELWAY BECAME "ELWAY"

John Elway's first three seasons saw glimpses of brilliance, but some inconsistency. In most eras of football, this sort of early-career trajectory was typical for a star quarterback in the making; the immediate star like Dan Marino was unusual. But Elway already had the knack for game-tying and game-winning drives in the fourth quarter and overtime down; in his first three seasons, he had ten such games with those heroics.

Joe Collier's defense offered a buffer for Elway's growth in those early years. But by 1986, Elway was maturing, taking over, and more often starting to carry the entire team on his broad shoulders. In that season, he accounted for twenty-one touchdowns—nineteen passing, one rushing, and one receiving, as the halfback option pass from Steve Sewell to the Elway became a favorite bold gambit of young offensive coordinator Mike Shanahan, who joined the staff in 1984 and became coordinator a year later.

By Week 9, the Broncos were 8-1 and had completed a season sweep of the Los Angeles Raiders with a 21-10 win at the Los Angeles Memorial Coliseum. Three years before, Raiders owner Al Davis had tried—and failed—to put together a package of players and draft picks to get into position to land Elway. Twice a year, Elway reminded the Raiders of what they missed out on.

"I didn't even see the ball. I barely saw the blur," Raiders cornerback Lester Hayes told *Sports Illustrated* at the time. "He nailed me. Elway's unstoppable. If he's healthy, Denver goes 15-1. He does things I've never seen before, and I've got lots of film."

Added Raiders linebacker Rod Martin: "The legs are like (Fran) Tarkenton's. The arm's all his."

The complete package at quarterback carried the Broncos to its second AFC West title in three years and a divisional-round showdown with the New England Patriots, the defending AFC champions.

A PRICELESS FREE PLAY

Elway wasn't just an elite athlete playing quarterback, but he played with intelligence that became more apparent with every year. By 1986, he was one of the smartest quarterbacks in the game, and his quick thinking provided one of the biggest plays in the Broncos' first playoff win in nine years.

It was the last play of the third quarter, and the Broncos had third-and-4 at the New England 48-yard-line. Patriots linebacker Don Blackmon stepped offside, Elway quickly called for the snap,

Getting the ball to Vance Johnson was never the intention—until Blackmon jumped.

"I knew where I was going as soon as I saw Blackmon offside," Elway said.

"Vance was not the primary receiver," Reeves added. "It was a smart play. It was John's option after he saw the offsides."

Johnson adjusted his route while the ball was in mid-flight, caught it at the goal line and put the Broncos in front to stay. But Johnson insisted that he adjusted to the position of Patriots cornerback Ernest Gibson and not to the ball.

"He had to adjust to me, not the ball. I adjusted to him," Johnson said.

A Rulon Jones safety with 1:37 left would clinch the 22-17 win that answered the growing questions of Reeves and Elway about whether they could win in the postseason after defeats in 1983 and 1984.

"I feel pleased (and) overjoyed," Reeves said. "The fact that we were 0-2 in the playoffs—people seem to remember that more than anything else."

What people also forget about Elway's first postseason win is the pain he was in. Elway sprained his ankle in the second quarter but returned for the second half.

"At halftime, the medicine man put some stuff on my ankle," Elway said, referring to long-time head athletic trainer Steve Antonopulos. "He said, 'If this is going to work, it better work now.'"

"I told John at the half if he could go, fine. But we could put Gary (Kubiak, the backup quarterback) in there," Reeves added. "But he said, 'Let me try it.'"

It worked perfectly, setting up a day that would define Elway.

"The Drive"

In the fourth quarter of the 1986 AFC Championship, a game with pendulum swings of momentum finally appeared to be locked in the direction of the homestanding Cleveland Browns. They had scored 10 consecutive points, and had taken a 20-13 lead on a 48-yard pass from Bernie Kosar to Brian Brennan. The Broncos had gone three-and-out on their previous two series.

History was about to be made. But before that could happen, the Broncos' situation got worse.

As often happens, it took a bizarre set of circumstances to create a moment for the ages. A horrendous, 49-yard kickoff by Cleveland's Mark Moseley that hit the ground at the Denver 16-yard-line, in front of returner Ken Bell. A bad bounce that sent the ball careening to Bell's right and past him inside the 5-yard-line before he could corral it. And finally, the ball squirting through Bell's hands as he tried to lean down to field it, leaving him to fall on the football inside the Denver 2-yard-line.

Ninety-eight yards to go. Five minutes and 34 seconds, remaining.

"I thought it was all over," Broncos owner Pat Bowlen would later recall to NFL Films. "I had left the visiting owners' box to come down to the field, just about the time they kicked off. When I saw the ball on the 2-yard-line, I thought, oh, my God. First of all, we're not going to get out of our own end zone."

In the Broncos' huddle, tension grew along with the noise from 79,915 fans yelling, barking, and brandishing Milk-Bones in honor of their beloved "Dawg Pound" defense. At that point, left guard Keith Bishop spoke up.

"We have them right where we want them," he said.

"I'm thinking, 'Are you kidding me?'" right tackle Dave Studdard recalled to *The Denver Post* in 2012.

But what Bishop said was exactly what the Broncos needed: a little bit of deadpan, but with some honest truth behind it. There was more than five minutes left, so there was plenty of time. And without the confidence to believe the job could be done, how could the Broncos be successful?

"I don't know if there was a fear, or an intense confidence in my eyes. When you looked around the huddle, I think everyone had confidence in them, but it was mixed with just enough fear to make us play well."

"Honestly, I felt like we had a chance. Anytime you have a John Elway as your quarterback, you have a chance," said Reeves. "I could see the determination in his eyes."

Added wide receiver Steve Watson to *Sports Illustrated*: "In the huddle after that kickoff to the two (-yard-line) he [Elway] smiled—I couldn't believe it—and he said, 'If you work hard, good things are going to happen.' And then he smiled again."

The first step was the smallest: get out of the shadow of the uprights. With the ball at the 2-yard-line, even a holding penalty could have ended the game, since it would have been in the end zone, resulting in a safety. One play, mission accomplished, as Elway found Sammy Winder on a five-yard swing pass. Two more carries by Winder moved the ball to the Denver 12, and moved the chains.

The Broncos had downs, and breathing room. Now, they could finally begin running their offense. After another Winder gain of three yards, Elway began gaining yards in clumps: 11 yards on a scramble, 22 yards on a pass to Steve Sewell, 12 yards on a toss to Steve Watson. The Broncos were in Cleveland territory at the Browns 40-yard-line, and their still-raucous fans began squirming at the two-minute warning.

Then, the Browns rallied. An incompletion, a sack by Dave Puzzoli, and the Broncos were back in desperate straits again: at the Cleveland 48, facing third-and-18. The despair heightened for a split second at the shotgun snap, which bounced off Watson, in motion to the right side. But the ball bounced off him and fluttered to Elway, who leaned forward to catch the football.

After that, the play proceeded exactly as it was drawn. Elway stepped back and had plenty of time; the Browns had only rushed three defenders, and Denver's offensive line easily kept the pocket pristine.

Mark Jackson had worked past Hanford Dixon and was wide open under the Browns' zone coverage. Even though he had not caught a pass all game, he was Elway's primary read. It was as easy as a high-pressure, long-yardage play can be. Jackson grabbed the pass, fell forward one yard and had the 20-yard gain to the Cleveland 28.

That was the last third-and-long the Broncos saw. An incompletion was followed by a 14-yard screen pass to Sewell. Another incompletion preceded a nine-yard Elway scramble, setting up third-and-1 at the Cleveland 5-yard-line with 39 seconds remaining. From there, Elway took the snap, dropped back to the 16-yard-line and found Jackson on a slant route for the touchdown that, along with Rich Karlis' extra point, forced overtime.

"When our backs are closest to the wall is when we really play our best—and we couldn't get any closer to the wall," Elway said after the game.

"The day before a big game, you dream of doing things like that."

A dream, but in a nightmarish set of circumstances. A hostile crowd throwing dog biscuits in honor of their beloved "Dawg Pound" defense. Frigid temperatures and a wind blowing from Lake Erie. A field that was grass in name only; by mid-January in northeast Ohio, it was scarcely more than painted dirt.

But it would take another possession for "The Drive" to become legend, and not a footnote.

THE NEXT DRIVE, THEN THE KICK

The Broncos lost the coin toss to begin the sudden-death period by calling heads. But with the Browns in third-and-2, budding star Karl Mecklenburg fought through the block of Cleveland guard Dan Fike to obstruct Herman Fontenot on a carry to the right side. Rulon Jones closed from the back side, and the Broncos had forced the three-and-out that nullified the coin toss.

Denver's overtime drive didn't begin with the same adversity as the march in regulation, but it had equal drama—never more than on third-and-12 from the 50-yard-line. Elway took the shotgun snap and dropped back to the Denver 38-yard-line. But unlike most of his passes during "The Drive," the Browns brought pressure, and Elway was forced to scramble to his left, eluding Carl Hairston and Sam Clancy. As Elway approached the line of scrimmage near the left sideline, it looked as though he might run. Then he spotted Watson 30 yards downfield and straight ahead of him.

He fired one of his customary bullets. Watson leapt and snatched the pass. Safety Felix Wright arrived a split-second too late to prevent the 28-yard gain to the Cleveland 22.

"That was vintage Elway," Watson said after the game. "Not many quarterbacks would have had the composure to see my man (Cleveland cornerback Hanford Dixon) had left me. But he did, and that's why he's such a great quarterback."

Three handoffs to Winder followed, advancing the Broncos to the Cleveland 15.

"Just like practice. Just like practice," teammates told Karlis as he walked onto the field, cleat on his left foot, his right foot bare to the elements—for the biggest kick in Broncos history.

"I tried to remember that when I went out there. It was just like one of those Fridays when we practice our game-winners," he said a few minutes later.

But when the ball soared toward the left goalpost, Karlis did not know if it was inside the uprights. It sailed high of the goalposts, leaving a judgment call for field judge Johnny Grier.

"I wasn't sure if I had made it at first," Karlis said in the locker room. "I couldn't have made it by more than a foot."

In Cleveland, fans will still lament that the football actually sailed wide left. But the man with the best view was Grier, who later went on to become a referee heading up an officiating crew for seventeen seasons. He pointed his arms toward the gray sky, and Karlis, holder Gary Kubiak, and their teammates jumped for joy. The image of their celebration was captured for posterity on the cover of *Sports Illustrated.* Instant replay, which was in its first year of its initial form, could not overturn the call. Denver was Super Bowl-bound.

"When you make 'em like that, it only makes it more exciting," Karlis said.

BAREFOOT IN THE GRASS

Like Members Only jackets, hair metal, and breakdancing, barefoot placekickers were a peculiar 1980s trend. With the exception of a brief shoeless experiment by the St. Louis Rams' Jeff Wilkins in 2002, it has been nearly two decades since a barefoot kicker or punter worked consistently in the NFL, and a quarter-century since there were a handful of bare feet at once on NFL rosters.

It was an odd sight. Denver's Rich Karlis, the survivor of a 478-player open tryout in 1982 that included 75 placekickers, handled kickoffs and placekicks with nothing on his right foot and ankle. Mike Lansford, then of the Los Angeles Rams, would don a shoe and a sock only for kickoffs.

In Karlis' seven seasons in orange and blue, he was subjected to endless questions about kicking barefoot, whether he was talking with the media or mingling at parties.

"All the time, the same thing: 'Does it hurt to kick barefoot? Does it hurt to kick barefoot? Does it hurt to kick barefoot?' They must think I'm into sadomasochism," Karlis said in 1988. "Yeah, that's it. I think that's what I'll say from now on. 'Yeah, it hurts like crazy! And I love it!'

"Of course it doesn't hurt. It did when I first started out. But it also taught me to concentrate more. Even in winter games, I became more careful about what I was doing than a lot of guys wearing shoes."

Only a barefoot kicker would slather cream manufactured for horse's hooves on his foot. The cream, he told *The New York Times* in 1987, was to prevent calluses on his feet from cracking. It worked so well that by the time his seven-year run in Denver ended, he was the second-leading scorer in franchise history; to this day, he still ranks fourth.

The Sunset of the Orange Crush

Nine years and ten days after the Broncos' only previous Super Bowl trip in January 1978, the Broncos were back—but the last vestiges of the original Orange Crush that powered Denver to Super Bowl XII were aging fast. Nose tackle Rubin Carter, who suffered a knee injury early in 1986, was supplanted by young, 255-pound Greg Kragen and retired. Linebacker Tom Jackson and safety Steve Foley would retire after Super Bowl XXI; cornerback Louis Wright packed it in during training camp in 1987.

For these seasoned pros, the Hollywood ending would have involved shutting down the Giants' conservative, power-running offense, giving Elway the chances he needed to mount a scoring drive or two, and then intercepting Giants quarterback Phil Simms to seal a Super Bowl win. But the Giants flipped the script, and the Broncos' defense was left winded.

Instead of sticking with their usual tactics, the Giants used the run to set up Phil Simms' pinpoint passing. He completed 88 percent of his 25 throws—still an NFL postseason record—and surgically diced Denver's defense, which was not expecting the

Giants to emphasize the pass and for the previously inconsistent Simms to be so accurate. Simms redefined his career and legacy and the Broncos were left with their second Super Bowl defeat in two trips.

That the Giants had beaten Denver in the regular season served as a cold reminder that they were a better team. There was no shame in that 39-20 defeat, and the Broncos were unmistakably headed in the right direction. Elway was already elite, and the team could look forward to many more years of championship contention.

But the defense was headed toward a period of transition. While stars like Mecklenburg, Rulon Jones, and Dennis Smith remained to anchor the unit, it would be a couple of years until it resembled its former self on a consistent basis.

STRIKE, TAKE TWO

The wounds of the 1982 work stoppage had barely healed when rumblings of a strike after two weeks of the 1987 season began to grow. But this time, the owners intended to keep playing with replacement teams. Many of the "B" teams were composed of training-camp cuts who had some familiarity with the playbook and the coaches, but those weren't enough to fill out any roster, leading to a flood of semi-pros, former USFL prospects, and some who'd played that summer in a four-team Arena Football League which had its first, "showcase" season of 50-yard football.

Some were even NFL players who came out of retirement for one last cameo. One such player was running back Nathan Poole, who played for the Broncos in 1982, 1983, and 1985. Poole returned after pursuing a career as a professional bodybuilder and ran for 126 yards and a touchdown during his two weeks back.

"I really hadn't given a thought to coming back," Poole admitted.

But the star of the temporary Broncos was running back Joe Dudek, who had been cut in training camp earlier that summer. Two years earlier, Dudek was playing at Division III Plymouth State in New Hampshire and was featured on the cover of *Sports Illustrated* as "The Thinking Fan's Vote for the 1985 Heisman Trophy." After a 40-10 loss to the Houston Oilers in the first week of replacement play, Dudek had his breakout game: 128 yards and two touchdowns in a 30-14 dismantling of the Los Angeles Raiders.

Befitting Dudek's knack at letting the big stage come to him, his performance came on *Monday Night Football* in front of 61,230—a smaller crowd than usual at Mile High Stadium but one that dwarfed other stadia around the league. Some crowds during replacement play were announced at less than 5,000. The Broncos averaged 49,862 for their two strike home games.

"It shows me how much Denver loves the Broncos," Reeves said. "I realize that there were mixed emotions out there, but we had great support."

Of course, it was the Raiders. And it was a game that counted in the standings. Heading into the contest, the Broncos were 1-1-1 and trailed their arch-rivals by a half-game in the standings. The win sent the teams in opposite directions; the Raiders lost seven in a row, while the Broncos won seven of their next nine games to earn their third AFC West title in four seasons.

RIGHT PLACE, RIGHT TIME

Jeremiah Castille had been unwanted by the hapless Tampa Bay Buccaneers, so he arrived in Denver in 1987 as a waiver claim with few expectations and even less fanfare. He was around to provide depth, and that was expected to be all for the former University of Alabama standout.

Instead, he made one of the greatest defensive plays in Broncos history, alertly stripping the football from Browns running back Earnest Byner when he was en route to a game-tying touchdown late in the 1987 AFC Championship at Mile High Stadium. Castille forced the fumble and then recovered it, providing yet another nail of heartbreak in Cleveland's coffin of football despair.

Unlike the previous year at Municipal Stadium, it was the Browns who had built a cresting tide of momentum late in the game. Denver had led 21-3 at halftime, but from that point forward the Browns were nearly unstoppable, sprinting to four consecutive touchdowns before the Broncos finally forced a punt with the score tied at 31. The Broncos seized the lead back on a 20-yard Elway-to-Sammy Winder pass with 4:01 remaining, but the Browns quickly struck back, mixing Byner's carries with a pair of Bernie Kosar completions.

With seventy-two seconds left and the Browns at the Denver 8-yard-line, Kosar handed it to Byner once more. The path to the south end zone was wide open.

"I was scared to death," Elway said.

"I didn't hold out a lot of hope when I saw Byner running for the end zone with the ball," added linebacker Jim Ryan.

"From where he was, I thought he was going to score," Reeves said. "I was really thinking about who was going to win the coin toss for overtime. Whoever got the ball first was going to win the game."

Then Castille intervened.

"I saw it loose and one of our guys fell on it, and I just said, 'Thank you, Lord.'"

Castille, was always reluctant to talk with reporters, and that remained the case after the game when he declined interview requests.

"He's not talking to you guys? What are you doing to my players? He was a nice guy when you came here," Reeves joked.

But those good feelings vanished a fortnight later during Super Bowl XXII. After taking a 10-0 lead on the Washington Redskins, the Broncos collapsed. That Doug Williams and Washington played arguably the best 15 minutes of offensive football in NFL history was of no consolation, and the Broncos absorbed a 42-10 defeat that wiped away the warm feelings of a second consecutive AFC title and Elway's league MVP trophy.

A Selection to Forget

There are draft busts, and then there is the unfortunate tale of Ted Gregory, the Broncos' first-round pick with the 27th overall selection in 1988. He is one of two first-round picks since the institution of the common draft in 1967 to never play for the Broncos, but the other, Chris Hinton, had a good reason: he was traded to the Baltimore Colts in the Elway deal just days after Denver selected him with the fourth overall pick.

Gregory was damaged goods when the Broncos picked him; he had knee problems the previous two years at Syracuse University. Unsurprisingly, he had more knee problems during training camp.

A decade later, Gregory would admit to taking steroids during his senior season at Syracuse. He rationalized it because he felt he needed to get bigger for the NFL to notice him.

"A 6-foot-1, 255-pound nose tackle isn't going to be a first-round pick, so I took something to get to 270," Gregory said in 1998.

But he wasn't 6-foot-1. He was actually two inches shorter—or more, depending on who you asked. That didn't help matters. Neither did the fact that he was a poor fit for the Broncos' scheme.

"It's hard to play two-gap when you've been playing one-gap," director of player personnel Reed Johnson said at the time.

After five weeks, Gregory was dealt to the New Orleans Saints for defensive tackle Shawn Knight—a first-round pick in 1987 also considered a bust.

Gregory only had one moment of NFL glory—ironically enough, against the Broncos, when he posted his first and only pro sack, taking down Elway for a loss. He reinjured his knee later in the Saints' 42-0 beatdown of the Broncos and never played again.

END OF AN ERA

The 42 points allowed in the Louisiana Superdome on November 20, 1988, were part of a troubling pattern for Joe Collier's defense. After allowing 14.4 points per game in the first seven weeks, Denver allowed 27.9 points a game in the last nine, including 42 points twice and 55 points to the Indianapolis Colts on Halloween. The Broncos finished 22nd in the league in yardage allowed, and the 352 points conceded was the most in twenty years, and particularly galling to a club that prided itself on its defense.

The manner in which the Broncos were gashed by the Redskins in Super Bowl XXII still stung, too. A day after the Broncos concluded their disappointing 8-8 season, Collier and four defensive assistants were sacked, including linebacker coach Myrel Moore and defensive line coach Stan Jones, both of whom had been with the team since the John Ralston era.

Collier served twenty years as a Broncos assistant; Jones was on the staff for eighteen seasons, including a five-year stint under Lou Saban. They remain the longest-serving assistant coaches in Broncos history, and with the pressure and instability of coaching in the NFL today, their records appear unlikely to be approached. Together, they helped define the playing philosophy of the Broncos for decades. Jones died in 2010, but Collier remains close to the organization and serves on the Ring of Fame selection committee.

Collier remains one of the most accomplished coordinators in NFL history, and if the Pro Football Hall of Fame ever decided to open its doors to coaches based on their accomplishments as assistants, he would undoubtedly be on the short list for induction.

WATCH THOSE WHITE HOUSE MEALS

On November 20, 1989, the Broncos were in Washington to face the Redskins, but their quarterback was in the bathroom, dealing with gastrointestinal discomfort. Elway had visited the White House briefly during the trip and ate chipped beef on toast, which rendered him ill and unable to play. (In general, "bad chipped beef on toast" is probably something of a redundant phrase; there's a reason its nickname in the U.S. military is ... well, something not fit for human consumption "on a shingle.")

Fortunately, the Broncos had Gary Kubiak, who came into the league in 1983 along with Elway. In his nine-year Broncos career, Kubiak was a credible 3-2 as a starter. This night at Washington was one of his three wins; he piloted the Broncos to a 14-10 triumph that was their only win at RFK Stadium. He threw two touchdown passes and led the final drive, a march that consumed the last six minutes and 45 seconds, allowing Denver to escape.

The Broncos would have eventually clinched home-field advantage in the AFC playoffs without the win; their 11-5 record was a game and a half better than No. 2 seed Cleveland in a weak year for the AFC. But Kubiak's performance proved the value of having an unfazed backup who knew the offense as well as the starter. Kubiak knew and accepted his role, and in doing so became a key part of the Broncos' legacy, which only increased when he returned in 1995 for a ten-year hitch on the coaching staff as Mike Shanahan's offensive coordinator.

ANOTHER SAD SUPER BOWL

The NFC had been pulling away from the AFC for five years, but 1989 probably represented the farthest the conferences sat from each other in terms of quality, at least in terms of their elite members. Seven NFC teams won at least ten games; the Broncos were the only AFC team to break double digits. The five NFC playoff teams went 16-4 against the AFC; the AFC's postseason quintet finished just 12-8.

Factor all that with a Super Bowl matchup between a team that had won three Super Bowls in the 1980s against a team that had lost two of the previous three, and the ingredients for a disaster were in place. The 49ers were 12-point favorites in Super Bowl XXIV, but by halftime, that prediction seemed quaint; they were up 27-3 and won 55-10 in the most lopsided margin in Super Bowl history.

The Broncos' third Super Bowl loss in four seasons was too much to bear. Some frustrated fans even burned their Broncos gear in front of television cameras. Elway was hounded by the 49ers' pass rush, and the balanced offense that powered the Broncos in the regular season and AFC playoffs was gone by the Super Bowl, with Bobby Humphrey unable to run.

Twenty-seven years later, this defeat—and the two in the Super Bowl before it—still rankled Elway. After the Broncos lost Super Bowl XLVIII in Elway's third year as an executive, he was asked how long it took to get over a Super Bowl loss.

Replied the Hall of Famer: "I'm not over them yet."

CHAPTER FOUR

The 1990s

The Broncos' fourth decade began with the franchise nursing a worse hangover than anything anyone has endured from a long night of Bourbon Street barhopping.

The 55-10 defeat to the San Francisco 49ers in Super Bowl XXIV was the franchise's fourth Super Bowl loss. At that juncture, this was a dubious distinction; only the Minnesota Vikings had lost four times without a win. The Buffalo Bills would join this club four years later. All were pegged as losers, a harsh and unfair critique given that they had made the Super Bowl four times in the first place. At the time the Broncos lost Super Bowl XXIV, ten teams had never made the Super Bowl; it was teams like the Cardinals, Buccaneers, and Falcons that should have been pegged as "losers," not a four-time AFC champion.

But that's the way it is for teams. It's exacerbated for quarterbacks and head coaches. And after the latest blowout, Elway and Reeves were each 0-3 in the biggest of games, which hung around each of them like a necklace made of lead.

"Whether it's fair or not, that's the way it is, and that's the way it's always going to be," Elway would reflect nearly a quarter-century later. "I think that is part of the position. It's going to be tied in with a head coach. You get quarterbacks that coach on the field. So head coaches and quarterbacks are tied together in the fact that statistics are nice, but the great ones are the ones that have won world championships."

THE VOICE, SILENCED

The biggest loss for the Broncos in the winter of 1990 wasn't the 55-10 defeat to the San Francisco 49ers in Super Bowl XXIV, but the death of radio play-by-play broadcaster Bob Martin, who had been the voice of the Broncos since 1970.

Cancer was engulfing Martin by the time the Broncos arrived in New Orleans for the Super Bowl, but he made the trip and intended to announce the game, just as he had called games throughout the season while battling his illness. But he took a turn for the worse in the team hotel the night before the game and was whisked away to a local hospital.

Twenty-nine days later, Martin died at fifty-seven.

Martin was not a typical football broadcaster. He was a classical music aficionado; he often attended symphony performances while on road trips, including one in Cleveland the night before the 1986 AFC Championship Game. He collected paintings and sculptures. He was as much a newsman as a sportscaster and was a mainstay on Denver's KOA radio discussing the Broncos, local politics, and everything in between.

And while he was clearly for the Broncos, he wasn't an over-the-top homer. He called the game as it was. His calls were elegant, energetic, but simple and clear. Never was that more the case than as the

1977 AFC Championship ended, when Martin spoke for an entire region of fans: "The miracle has happened! The Broncos are going to the Super Bowl!"

If you visit the studios of KOA in the Denver Tech Center ten miles south of downtown, you'll walk past shelves encased in glass that are filled with mementoes of the station's long history with Denver sports teams. The one that always catches my eye is the picture of a billboard erected to honor Martin at his passing. There's also a plaque in the press box at Sports Authority Field at Mile High to honor him, along with long-time *Denver Post* writer Dick Connor. These are small tributes, but they ensure that Martin remains unforgettable nearly twenty-five years after his last play-by-play call.

Changing Addresses

By the 1980s, the Broncos had outgrown the facility on the north side of Denver they had called home since 1969. Most of the football operations had moved to a new building across Logan Street from the main headquarters. The locker room was in another building entirely.

It was time to bid north Denver goodbye and move into the modern age of pro football: one in which the entire operations of a club could be conducted from one concentrated spot. Thus, the Broncos abandoned their home of twenty-two years at 5700 Logan Street and moved twenty-two miles southeast to a windswept stretch of prairie that was just being developed. The general area was called "Dove Valley," and, like "Valley Ranch" outside of Dallas, it has come to be a quick description of an NFL team's home.

The $8 million facility housed the entire Broncos organization until Sports Authority Field was constructed; after it opened, the marketing and stadium operations departments moved downtown, leaving team and football operations, public relations, some executive management, and finance at Dove Valley.

The only glaring negative about the new location was that its high prairie location turned into the NFL's biggest wind tunnel if the conditions were right. This was never more apparent than during an off-season practice in 2010, when sustained winds of 45 miles per hour buffeted the fields and even toppled one of the twenty-year-old evergreens near the practice field. Passes sailed high and wide of their targets. The two punters on the roster, Britton Colquitt and A.J. Trapasso, had fun with it; they started punting with the wind at their back and repeatedly uncorked blasts that sailed 80 to 90 yards in the air.

In 2013, it surpassed the north Denver building as the longest-serving day-to-day home of the Broncos. In that same year, a massive redevelopment of the facility was finalized, including a reconstruction of conference rooms, a new lobby in which the franchise's trophies will be prominently displayed, and most visibly, a massive field house on the west side of the complex in which the Broncos can hold full-field indoor practices for the first time. Proving how much times have changed, the project costs $35 million—more than four times as much as the initial construction.

Atwater Ends the "Nightmare"

No matter how many more hits Steve Atwater made in his career after the 1990 season, it was his right-shoulder shiver to the Kansas City Chiefs' Christian Okoye that came to define his legacy.

Atwater gave up 42 pounds to the 260-pound Okoye, who earned his "Nigerian Nightmare" nickname by melding 4.4 speed with bruising power. In 1989, it was Okoye, and not future Hall of

Famer Barry Sanders, who had led the league in rushing and there was a legitimate debate as to which running back was better and would last longer.

The Broncos won the *Monday Night Football* showdown, 24-23, Okoye was never quite the same after that. In his previous 16 games, he'd broken the 100-yard mark eight times. He had just four 100-yard games in the next 39 games before his career ended after six seasons.

"Yeah, you tried, baby," Atwater said, standing over the suddenly humbled running back. Atwater had been mic'd up by NFL Films for the game.

But he was as steady as he was spectacular. He read plays well and rarely missed tackles. He melded the potential for massive hits with sound tackling. He learned from veteran and fellow Ring of Famer Dennis Smith, then carried the secondary after Smith retired following the 1994 season.

A Fall, and Then a Quick Rise

"Can the Broncos snap out of their Super Bowl stupor?" read the headline in *Sports Illustrated's* August 13, 1990, edition.

After the Broncos' first two Super Bowl defeats, they rebounded with vigor, winning the AFC West in 1978 and the conference in 1987. The third Super Bowl loss was followed by an 8-8 finish in which they missed the playoffs by just one game, but didn't quit; in fact, their motivation was so strong in Week 16 that they knocked the New England Patriots out of the postseason with a season-ending win.

But 1990 was different. After a 2-1 start, the Broncos lost two consecutive one-point games, at Buffalo and at home to the Browns, who claimed a tiny measure of revenge for the Broncos' three AFC Championship Game wins in the previous four seasons. Denver went 2-7 in games decided by a touchdown or less, including 0-for-their-last-6 in tight games. Only two wins in the last three games ended a 1-9 run and saved the Broncos from further embarrassment.

But the decline was short-lived. From the ashes of 5-11 came the best regular season since 1977, a 12-4 finish that vaulted the Broncos back to the top of the AFC West. The roster wasn't radically turned over, but the changes were apparent.

"A few key people and attitude," wide receiver Mark Jackson said in 1991. "Last year, we didn't have a terribly bad team, but we did have a terrible record. We kind of went down the tubes."

The 1991 Broncos won the close games the 1990 edition lost, going 8-3 in contests decided by seven points or less. Their proficiency in those games would set up another dramatic, franchise-defining playoff victory.

"THE DRIVE, II"

On January 4, 1992, John Elway and the Broncos faced first-and-10 at their own 2-yard-line. Sounds familiar, right? But even though the Broncos trailed the Houston Oilers by a solitary point, they had over three minutes less time than they did five years earlier at Cleveland's Municipal Stadium.

The Broncos did not have to march 98 yards in 5:32. But they did need to go at least 60 yards in two minutes to give David Treadwell a plausible shot at the game-winning field goal. And unlike January 1987, the Broncos were out of timeouts.

"There are times when you know the situation is hopeless," said wide receiver Michael Young. "But one look at John, and we knew we had a chance."

With less time on their hands, Elway and the Broncos did not have the luxury of calling short passes and handoffs to escape the end zone:

they had to move, now. Under a four-man rush, Elway dropped eight yards into the end zone, and fired a strike to Young. The pass covered 22 yards, and the Broncos were at their 24 at the two-minute warning.

Then, the drive stalled. The aggressive, versatile Oilers brought seven pass rushers on first down, four on second down with a linebacker in contain, and six on third down, when Elway completed a four-yard pass to Ricky Nattiel. With fourth-and-6, the Oilers only rushed three men, dropping seven into deep coverage, and one man into close containment. No one was open, but Elway escaped the pocket, sprinted to the left sideline and got out of bounds—two steps beyond the first-down marker.

But that was only a temporary reprieve. The Oilers kept mixing up their packages, alternating blitzes and tight coverages. Elway's next three passes fell incomplete; one was deflected at the line of scrimmage. With 59 seconds remaining, the Broncos had another fourth down.

Houston called timeout. At the snap, the defense rushed four men. Elway waited, and then stepped up in the pocket, moving toward the left sideline—just like he had on the previous fourth down. The threat of Elway's legs sustaining the drive brought cornerback Richard Johnson forward. Eight yards behind him and near the sideline was Vance Johnson.

Instead of using the howitzer, Elway lofted the pass toward Vance Johnson, and over the cornerback's flailing, desperate hand. The pass was caught, and the Broncos' Johnson turned upfield past mismatched Oilers linebacker Al Smith and didn't stop until he'd sprinted 29 yards after the catch, for a 44-yard gain to the Houston 21-yard-line.

"Sometimes, they lose guys when John starts scrambling," Vance Johnson noted. "If John Elway is not running for a first down, he's going to find someone."

Mile High erupted. Elway's teammates rejoiced, a mixture of giddiness and awe.

"This has got to be the most amazing thing I've ever seen," Kubiak said after the game. "Everything we did was improvising, once John started on the final drive. He was something. I'm just glad he's on my side."

But you wouldn't have read all that if Gary Kubiak, Elway's long-time understudy, had not made one of the greatest holds on a field-goal attempt in NFL history. Kubiak had mishandled a snap on a first-quarter extra point, accounting for the 24-23 deficit the Broncos faced as Elway went to work.

But on David Treadwell's 28-yard field goal attempt, Kubiak saved the season by fielding a shaky snap from the injured Keith Kartz, then quickly spinning it into position as Treadwell's foot arrived. The kick sailed through the south uprights, and now the home fans at Mile High Stadium could say they bore witness to one of the signature drives in NFL history.

"I just smothered it and put it down after trapping it," said Kubiak. "Keith couldn't play, but bless his soul, he could barely bend over, but he thought he could make the snap. I didn't look up once David started with his foot. But I saw it once it went through."

With less time, no timeouts, and two fourth downs, the Broncos' 12-play, 87-yard march was arguably more impressive than "The Drive."

"I was part of the Cleveland drive, but this one was nicer," said running back Steve Sewell. "Everyone wanted the ball on the last drive to make a play. We didn't mention Cleveland in the huddle."

The only thing missing? A player with a pithy, tension-breaking observation like Keith Bishop did in Cleveland.

"I was thinking of Bishop," said Elway. "I missed him saying, 'We've got them right where we want them.'"

Kubiak and Treadwell would play prominent roles eight days later in the AFC Championship Game against the Buffalo Bills, but not as they dreamed. On a windy afternoon, Treadwell missed three field-goal attempts. Kubiak replaced Elway, who suffered a right thigh injury, and nearly led a comeback, but a Sewell fumble ended the Broncos' late comeback hopes in a 10-7 loss.

Too Much Is Not a Good Thing

The Broncos' locker room was understandably jubilant after the comeback over the Oilers. As was—and is—custom after big wins, particularly in the postseason, NFL Films had a camera in the locker room to capture the emotion and postgame speeches.

But all wide receiver Vance Johnson wanted to do before marinating in the win was get changed out of his grass-stained, sweat-soaked uniform, shower, and freshen up. So as others celebrated, Johnson quietly disrobed. And that was the problem, because the camera captured it all—which was aired on *Inside the NFL* several days later.

"Unfortunately, it showed everything," said Mike Burg, an attorney retained by Johnson for a lawsuit.

This was long before TiVo and DVRs, so as I watched it on television, I saw the sight out of the corner of my eye and muttered, "Did I really just see what I thought I saw?"

Yep.

"It was certainly discernible to the public," Burg said at the time. "His mother-in-law had seen it. His sister had seen it."

Of course, this aired on HBO—so it was nothing that had not been seen on the network before, at least in the late-night hours. But it was hardly what viewers at 7 p.m. Eastern time expected.

Johnson sued HBO for invasion of privacy, outrageous conduct, defamation, and negligence, but he dropped the lawsuit two months later and settled out of court.

It was the most unusual incident in a life that has been unique and eventful. In 1996, he went on *The Oprah Winfrey Show* to admit that he abused his former wife and other women. Later in retirement, he grappled with alcoholism, for which he successfully sought treatment. Johnson's interests were all over the map; he ran a restaurant, practiced ballet during his career—which helped his strength and flexibility—and often found release through painting and drawing.

"I have something to escape with in my artwork," Johnson said during the Broncos' 1986 playoff run. "I draw all night sometimes. I can draw until 3 o'clock in the morning."

Because he could draw up the proper adjustments to cornerbacks and Elway's passes in flight, Johnson was the most prolific of the Three Amigos, catching 415 passes for 5,695 yards in ten Broncos seasons.

Two Quarterbacks Are Not Better Than One

When Elway suffered a right shoulder injury ten games into the 1992 season, the Broncos were 7-3 and looked to be rolling along to their eighth winning season and seventh playoff appearance in a decade. But behind the scenes, the ties between Elway and head coach Dan Reeves were fraying.

The Broncos had used their first-round pick that year on UCLA quarterback Tommy Maddox instead of drafting a wide receiver like Tennessee's Carl Pickens that Elway and the offense desperately needed to regenerate an aging corps that lacked an elite target. Mike Shanahan, who had returned to the Broncos as an assistant in 1989 after being fired by the Los Angeles Raiders after one and a quarter seasons as head coach, now worked for the San Francisco 49ers; he had been dismissed by Reeves after the 1991 season.

Maddox would eventually start in the NFL and win a playoff game. But that was a decade, four NFL teams, and three leagues away. In 1992, he looked out of his depth in his first two starts, which the Broncos lost by a combined 40-13 margin.

The Dallas Cowboys lurked in Week 14 and the Broncos' fading postseason hopes rested on an upset of the eventual world champions. Desperate for answers, Reeves turned back to a tactic he saw when working in Dallas under Tom Landry: he alternated quarterbacks on every play, exchanging Maddox for Shawn Moore.

"Rookies have so many things to think about," Reeves said. "I felt I'd give them a little more time to think about the execution, talking to them on the sideline from there to when they got in the huddle."

It got a bit awkward when the Broncos needed to run the two-minute offense; when that happened, each quarterback was given multiple plays so he could stay on the field until the clock stopped. With the Broncos trailing 31-27, Maddox ran two plays, Moore two, Maddox one, Moore two, and Maddox the last one—an interception by Cowboys cornerback Kenneth Gant with 1:16 left that squashed the upset threat. Maddox threw three touchdowns, but had four interceptions. Moore avoided the big mistakes and brought the threat of the run.

But the best passer that day was wide receiver and punt returner Arthur Marshall, who hit Cedric Tillman for an 81-yard touchdown. To this day, Marshall has the best quarterbacking career stat line in Broncos history: two completions on two attempts, 111 yards, two touchdowns, and a perfect 158.3 passer rating.

The Maddox/Moore rotation continued for another week, but Moore threw three interceptions in a loss at Buffalo. Elway returned for Weeks 16 and 17, but it was too little, too late; the Broncos split the games and finished 8-8.

One day later, Reeves was dismissed with barely a month left on his contract.

"Life goes on," said Reeves, who wasted no time landing the same job with the New York Giants. He would coach another eleven seasons in the NFL, go to the Super Bowl once more, and win four playoff games. But he never had another quarterback like Elway, and the slight decline in his results reflected that reality: then, as now, it's all about the quarterback.

WADE LIGHTENS THE MOOD

Wade Phillips first joined the Broncos in 1989 with two daunting tasks: rebuild a declining defense and successfully replace the best assistant coach the Broncos had ever known, long-time defensive coordinator Joe Collier.

Phillips was worthy. With the drafting of Steve Atwater revitalizing the defense, the unit finished in the league's top five two of Phillips' first three years on the job. After rumblings of interest in Shanahan, Pat Bowlen promoted Phillips to replace Dan Reeves, and there was some merit to the choice. Phillips was everything that Reeves was not by the time of his 1992 dismissal: gregarious, avuncular, easy-going.

"Is it different?" asked Elway during training camp. "Well, for one thing, it wasn't much of a day at camp [in 1992] if there weren't at least five or six fights. There's not all that tension out there this year, the fear for jobs. There's none of that intimidation."

Phillips hired Jim Fassel as offensive coordinator and opened up an often conservative attack; Elway responded with the best statistical season of his career to that point. The changes on the sideline re-energized No. 7; he seemed looser and more relaxed, and the offense allowed him to use his howitzer right arm more than ever before.

But after a 9-5 start to the 1993 season, fortunes began to turn against Phillips. On December 26, the woeful Tampa Bay Buccaneers strolled into Mile High Stadium on a Florida-like, 57-degree day and stunned the Broncos, 17-10. A week later, the Raiders came from behind for a 33-30 win that forced the wild card rematch one week later to be played in Los Angeles Memorial Coliseum. The second leg of the two-week series wasn't close; the Broncos fell, 42-24.

The skid continued into 1994 and included yet another loss to the Raiders, a 48-16 thrashing at Mile High Stadium. To commemorate the NFL's 75th anniversary, the teams wore throwback uniforms; unfortunately, the Mac Speedie-era throwbacks saw a dismal result similar to the outcomes of the mid-1960s.

It was as frustrating a season as the Broncos had endured. The 0-4 start remains the worst after four games in club history, and a midseason revival wasn't enough to salvage the campaign or Phillips' job. But when he was sacked just after the season, owner Pat Bowlen had the replacement already in mind—a former Broncos assistant still in the process guiding the league's most prolific offense to a world championship.

ENTER "THE MASTERMIND"

Mike Shanahan was the right man at the right time when the Broncos hired him in 1995. The NFL was changing. Free agency was creating a fluid market that few teams had discerned how to exploit. Offenses were becoming more aggressive in this era, with San Francisco's intricate West Coast attack and the early 1990's run-and-shoot philosophy of the Detroit Lions, Houston Oilers, and Atlanta Falcons beginning to scratch the surface of the type of pinball numbers that could be achieved in a game where rules increasingly hindered the defense.

But most importantly, Shanahan offered a change in stylistic direction. Dan Reeves and Wade Phillips would win more games than they lost as NFL head coaches in careers that eventually spanned decades. But neither had the technocratic chops of Shanahan, nor did they possess his experience in the 49ers organization of that era.

In the 1980s and 1990s, San Francisco raised the bar for professionalism and a detail-oriented approach, first under Bill Walsh and then with his successor, George Seifert. Shanahan joined the 49ers in 1992 after being fired by Reeves and immediately succeeded Mike Holmgren as offensive coordinator when the latter took the head coaching reins of the Green Bay Packers.

By January 1998, Shanahan and his predecessor would meet as head coaches in Super Bowl XXXII—Reeves was then coaching the Falcons—a collision that was perhaps the ultimate triumph of the 49ers' method and how it could be applied in other franchises with different organizational strengths and different players' skill sets.

When Shanahan worked in San Francisco, he helped get his former Broncos backup quarterback, Gary Kubiak, on the staff. Kubiak would follow him back to Denver as offensive coordinator and the two would create some of the league's most dynamic, productive offenses for the next eleven seasons. In eight of those years, the Broncos had one of the league's top five offenses; six times they were in the top three. Attention to detail was a primary reason why.

"Mike is a stickler for detail in everything he does and he teaches you how to prepare and how to not leave any stone unturned in what you do whether you're trying to win a football game or whatever you're trying to do in coaching. It's something he drives into you every day," Kubiak said. "I think that when you work for him it's something that you're going to learn right away or else you're not going to last very long."

Building Prosperity from the Ground Up

Shanahan brought the 49ers' West Coast scheme with him from San Francisco. That also meant a heavier emphasis on zone blocking than the Broncos had ever known, since it was what powered San Francisco's running game via the tutelage of long-time assistant coach Bobb McKittrick.

Alex Gibbs, who had worked with Shanahan under Dan Reeves from 1984-87, was tapped to teach zone blocking to a group of offensive linemen that featured a future Hall of Famer at left tackle (Gary Zimmerman), an unheralded second-year center (Tom Nalen), with the rest of the group fitting in the extremes.

The genius of zone blocking, when it worked, was in its simplicity. And although it would be tweaked throughout Shanahan's fourteen years in Denver, it was easy to recognize elements in 2005 that were used a decade earlier.

"You have to be committed to something in this game and when we run the ball, that's what we do, we're a zone scheme," Kubiak said in 2005, a decade into his tenure as offensive coordinator. "Some teams may run forty or fifty various types of running plays a year. The Denver Broncos basically run four. We run a wide zone and a tight zone, right and left, so that's four.

"We do a lot of variations off of that, but the reason we do that is because we feel like we get numerous repetitions on something so we get good at doing that. We feel like if you run four and you run them over and over and over and over again—and you don't run 40 and run them once or twice a year—then you're getting good at something.

"The easiest way to explain it is we feel like it's simple. We feel like it adjusts to everything people do and we feel like it keeps us from wasting other plays and being committed to a scheme."

Shanahan, Kubiak, and Gibbs knew what they wanted. Now they needed to find the right running back. It took special teams to help reveal who that runner was.

TERRELL DAVIS: HUNGRY FROM THE START

The Broncos were regular overseas travelers for preseason games in the 1980s and 1990s, visiting London, Berlin, Barcelona, Tokyo, and Sydney for American Bowls played outside of North America. But no trip was more important to their future than the 1995 trek to Japan.

That's where the Broncos found the future star of their offense, running back Terrell Davis. He leapt up the depth chart after clobbering San Francisco's Tyronne Drakeford on a kickoff. But it almost didn't happen.

"You know the hit, but you don't know the story behind it, Davis said. "So it was the second preseason game in Tokyo. Well, the first preseason game, I didn't play (much). [He had one carry for no gain.] The second game, chances are I'm not going to play in the second game. It's past halftime and I'm hungry, man, I'm starving. So about the third quarter, I've got hot dogs, I've got chili dogs, I've got French fries, I've got ding dongs, I've got Snickers, thinking I'm not going to play.

"So, come the fourth quarter, they come to me—I think it was (assistant coach Richard Smith), who was a special teams coach, he said, 'Hey, we're going to put you in.' He asked me if I wanted to go in and I was thinking, 'Dude, I just ate all kinds of food, I don't know if I want to go in the game now.' The game was basically over, so I said, 'Okay, I'll go in.' So I went in, thank God I did, I went in and made that hit.

"So then I'm thinking that's the only play I'm going to play. Well, I come back to the sideline and running backs coach Bobby Turner comes over and says, 'Hey, we want you to play a few more snaps.' I threw up after I ran out on the kick. Bobby comes over and says, 'Are you okay?' 'Yeah, I'm fine Bobby.' 'Do you want to play?' 'Uh, sure man, I'll go in.' I went in and I think I had five runs or something like that. But that's where it all started.

"I think back to that because if I had said to (Coach) Smith that I didn't want to go in, who knows where I would be today? Again, it's because I'm over there eating hot dogs and stuff. So, kids, don't eat hot dogs when the opportunity presents itself—or Ding Dongs or Kit Kats or whatever else we had."

SNOW PROBLEM? NO PROBLEM

The 1997 Broncos may be the only group in history that flew to Buffalo to escape a snowstorm. A late-October storm dropped up to twenty inches of snow around the Denver area, making it nearly impossible for players to get to the facility without aid of at least a four-wheel drive—or, in some cases, snowmobiles.

Some players were prepared. Others, like cornerback Tim McKyer, were looking for the nearest heater so they could thaw. McKyer had to leave his car a block away from Dove Valley and didn't have any winter gear to protect himself.

"I was in my suit, and it was an adventure," he said. "The snow was high, and I had to run up on the median. Nobody was answering the door. My hands felt like mittens. I almost froze to death."

Local radio stations aired messages encouraging residents with any functional form of transportation to pick up the Broncos, who were stranded or still at home. The players and coaches finally made it to Dove Valley, and the convoy of buses trudged to Denver International Airport. Eight and a half hours late, the Broncos were finally airborne and didn't arrive in Buffalo until midnight the morning of the game. Despite the awful odyssey, the Broncos won, 23-20.

It wouldn't be the last time that snow affected the Broncos' plans under Shanahan. Nine years later, a mid-week snowstorm prior to a crucial Week 16 showdown with the Cincinnati Bengals not only kept the Broncos from being able to practice outside, but inside as well. Team buses couldn't make it one mile north on Broncos Parkway to the team's long-time alternate facility, the South Suburban Sports Dome, so the Broncos settled for two days of drills in their conditioning center, with a field barely large enough to simulate plays at half-speed. Players were late arriving at the facility as snowdrifts mounted.

Some coaches and staff didn't even bother going home during this storm, opting to ride it out at team headquarters. I chose this option and slept in an upstairs conference room. Work went on, but some were thrown off, including defensive tackle Gerard Warren, who declined an interview request thusly: "Please, please! There's a blizzard outside, I've got a bowl of potato soup and I'm stuck at the facility."

Despite the snow—and Warren's protestation—the Broncos won that game, too.

BRINGING BACK "ZIM"

The world-famous motorcycle rally in Sturgis, South Dakota, attracts thousands of riders. In the summer of 1997, one of them was left tackle Gary Zimmerman. At age thirty-five, he'd played thirteen seasons of pro football dating back to his days with the Los Angeles Express of the United States Football League and his left shoulder was in pain. Zimmerman had not filed his retirement papers by the time training camp opened in Greeley that July, but he wasn't with the Broncos; he was 363 miles north-northeast, in the Black Hills.

The Broncos were as close as they'd ever been to having a championship-worthy team. But it wasn't until Zimmerman agreed to return that the puzzle was complete. That was no easy task. In the off-season, he seemed as good as gone.

"I went and visited him and his wife up in their house in Oregon. I was on the way to a football camp down there and spent the night with him and he said, 'There's no way I'm coming back,'" recalled guard Brian Habib.

A few weeks later, Alex Gibbs stepped in.

"Coach Gibbs called to try to talk me into coming back for another season," Zimmerman said in 2003. "I knew I'd be coming back, but I wanted to find out how serious they were. So, I told him, 'If you guys are really serious about having me back, send Elway up here.'

"The next day, Elway was outside my tent."

Soon, he was back for one final run.

"We gave him a hard time; we fined him quite a bit that following week," Habib said. "We were so glad to have him back, though."

From the Ashes of Defeat, Greatness Rises

By Shanahan's second year, the offense was at full gallop. Davis had curbed his in-game snack cravings and was en route to a second consecutive 1,000-yard season. The Broncos wrapped up home-field advantage by bursting to a 12-1 start to the season.

Jacksonville changed that. The second-year expansion team was the roadblock on the freeway to the Super Bowl, a feisty bunch that was peaking at the perfect time. A 30-27 win at Mile High Stadium was their seventh consecutive triumph after a 4-7 start and temporarily left the Broncos in despair.

"We were 13-3 and didn't take care of business," tight end Shannon Sharpe said.

By this time, Elway was on his 14th season. Seven years had passed since his last Super Bowl. He would be thirty-seven by the 1997 season. There was urgency to win for him—and with him before the championship window closed.

The loss to the Jaguars could have sunk the Broncos emotionally but instead it provided them more motivation than any Broncos team had known.

"The one key ingredient that we had that kind of burned in our souls throughout the off-season before that year was that loss to Jacksonville," recalled linebacker Glenn Cadrez. "That was the key ingredient to our success that kept us wanting to stay in the weight room a little longer, wanting to stay in the film room a little longer, wanting to get every little detail right, so that when we walked on the field, we were so prepared that there was no denying us."

SADDLE UP AND RIDE

In many ways, that made the entire 1997 season a prelude. The Broncos didn't win the AFC West; that honor, and the No. 1 seed with it, went to 13-3 Kansas City. But when the Broncos began their postseason run with a wild-card rematch against the Jaguars, it felt as though the Broncos were favorites.

"Even though our record didn't indicate it going from 13-3 to 12-4, we felt we were a better football team than the previous year," recalled Sharpe. "Now it was just a matter of going out and showing we were in the playoffs."

Their mindset was at the intersection of swagger and experience. They had confidence, but knew the consequence of messing up. And they went into the postseason determined to not repeat the mistakes of the previous year.

For one thing, the Broncos were going to ride their strongest horse. And even though Elway was a Pro Bowl quarterback, that meant heavy doses of Terrell Davis in the December and January chill.

"I think Mike (Shanahan) made a conscious decision also that he wasn't going to make the mistake that we had made the year before in not giving T.D. the opportunity to carry the football," said Sharpe. "That game we lost to Jacksonville, I think T.D. only carried the ball fourteen times, but he was averaging almost seven yards a carry. Mike was thinking, 'You know what? If I get back in this situation, I'm going to give T.D. as many carries as he needs to make sure we don't fall back into that situation where we're going to lose a game.'"

The result was the greatest sustained postseason work for a running back in NFL history. Over the next two seasons, Davis would break 100 yards in every playoff game. It began in the Jaguars rematch of December 27, 1997, when he carried the football 31 times for 184 yards and two touchdowns. Backup Derek Loville added another 103 yards and two touchdowns on 11 carries, as the Broncos trampled Jacksonville, 42-10.

Davis had 101 yards and a touchdown a week later at Kansas City; that was enough in a punishing, 14-10 win at Arrowhead Stadium. He racked up 139 yards on 26 carries and scored once in the AFC Championship Game at Pittsburgh; again, the Broncos prevailed, 24-21.

It was called the "Revenge Tour," because the Broncos had lost to Jacksonville the previous January and the Chiefs and Steelers during the regular season. Only the Packers remained in Super Bowl XXXII, and once again, the Broncos rode Davis, only pausing when he was overcome by a migraine headache in the second quarter, limiting his use to that of a decoy.

By the second half at Qualcomm Stadium in San Diego, Davis had recovered and the offense began chugging. Davis capped two second-half drives with one-yard touchdown runs, the latter of which came with 1:45 remaining—and against a defense that appeared to be laying back to permit the score and give more time for a potential Brett Favre comeback.

THE MOMENT OF VICTORY: SEALING THE WORLD TITLE

Whether the Packers intentionally let Davis score the touchdown or actually played to stop him is a matter that will be debated. But all that mattered was that 1:45 remained on the clock for Favre and the Packers to mount one final rally against a defense that ranked fifth in the NFL in 1997. The success of coordinator Greg Robinson's defenses was usually predicated more on forcing turnovers rather than limiting yards. His 1997 defense could do both.

But in an end-game situation, the Broncos had to be careful. Favre and the Packers took possession at their 30-yard-line with 99 seconds remaining. It took just 35 seconds for the Packers to move 35 yards to the Denver 35-yard-line. Most of the yardage came from Dorsey Levens, who took a short pass from Favre and gained 22 yards after breaking a tackle attempt by linebacker John Mobley.

"I knew I had to make up for it somehow and I just wanted the opportunity to do that," Mobley recalled.

"That series when the defense was on the field—knowing what Brett Favre can do and knowing what kind of offense the Packers had—that probably took about two years off my life," Habib said.

Then, the defense stiffened. It forced a fourth-and-6 with 32 seconds left in regulation. Favre looked for Mark Chmura, but Mobley, the man who missed the tackle six plays earlier, got his hand to the football first.

"We had a bomb blitz," Mobley recalled a decade later. "That was kind of our all-out blitz. It was one-on-one; you get whatever man that you got. I knew I had Chmura. I knew he was going to run an option route. If I played him to the inside he was going to cut out and if I played him outside he was going to break in and just get past the chain and Brett was going to throw him the ball so I kind of fiddle-faddled and played cat-and-mouse with him the whole time. He didn't know if I was inside or outside. When he finally sat down I just jumped on him and got my hands in there and knocked the ball down."

As Mobley later said, the emotions were obvious: "Nothing but joy and jubilation."

"All of a sudden, we looked up at the scoreboard and it was like, 'Hey, it's over. We win!' I didn't think about it the play before—that if we knock this pass down and we get off the field, we win the game. I didn't think about that the whole time," Steve Atwater later recalled.

"So all of a sudden, right in an instant, it's like, 'Man, we are the champs.' I just can't explain that energy and the looks on everyone's faces that (said), 'Hey, we did it. We pulled together as a team, we had great leadership from the top all the way down to the bottom and we were able to do what we set out to do.' There's no greater feeling in this world."

Those feelings only grew stronger when Pat Bowlen received the Vince Lombardi Trophy and declared, "This one's for John!" and handed the cherished piece of silver to Elway. Colorado rejoiced. The Broncos' journey from the Quonset hut had finally reached the promised land.

Elway's Perfect Ending

Go out on a high note. Leave the audience wanting more. From Broadway shows to George Costanza telling a joke at Kruger

Industrial Smoothing, everyone with an audience aspires to depart the stage to a loud, appreciative ovation rather than pity, scorn, or relief.

Most endings are of the latter kind. In sports, we think of Willie Mays not getting to balls while with the New York Mets, or Joe Namath unable to avoid a pass rush while wearing the blue and yellow of the Los Angeles Rams. In Denver, fans recall two-time National League MVP Dale Murphy finding no power in his last-ditch attempt to get to 400 home runs with the Colorado Rockies, or former Cowboys star Tony Dorsett playing in 1988 without the breakaway speed that defined him for eleven Hall of Fame-worthy seasons in Dallas.

That's what made Super Bowl XXXIII so special for the Broncos, Elway, and their fans. The greatest player the team had ever known, and arguably the greatest quarterback in the game's history, had the ride-off-into-the-sunset-on-a-white-horse finale that would have been rejected by a Hollywood producer as too hackneyed. And that was even without considering that the Broncos defeated the Atlanta Falcons, who were led by Reeves, the coach who once considered trading Elway.

The Broncos won, 34-19, in a game that was not as close as the score indicated. One was nice. Twice was a dynasty, putting the Broncos alongside the 1966-67 Packers, 1972-73 Dolphins, 1975-76 and 1979-80 Steelers, 1988-89 49ers, and 1992-93 Cowboys. The 2004-05 Patriots would join the club later.

Elway won the game's MVP award. Bowlen held aloft his second Lombardi Trophy, turned to the Broncos fans at Pro Player Stadium, and declared, "This one's for you!"

When Elway retired three months later, it was emotional, but it wasn't a surprise. Injuries and the accumulation of wear from a life spent playing football had exacted a toll. The only mountain left to climb would have been leading the Broncos to a third consecutive NFL title, which would have made them the first team to accomplish such a feat since the 1965-67 Green Bay Packers. But in the previous two years, Elway had proven with trophies that he had the championship mettle that many so long ago predicted.

1999: One Injury After Another

It seems hard to believe in retrospect, but the Broncos were tipped by many pundits as a Super Bowl contender in 1999 even though Elway had retired. During the 1998 season, the Broncos played without Elway in four games, starting Bubby Brister. But the offense rolled along unaffected, averaging 31.5 points a game and winning by an average of 21.8 points in those games.

The defense returned intact and added former Chiefs cornerback Dale Carter. All the other key skill components on offense returned: Rod Smith, Ed McCaffrey, Shannon Sharpe, Terrell Davis. The notion of a "three-peat" was in the air.

But the first earthquake hit when Shanahan opted to start Brian Griese ahead of Brister as the season dawned. There were perfectly logical reasons for this: Griese was regarded as the quarterback of the future, whereas Brister would merely be a bridge to it; Griese had a higher ceiling and would presumably only improve with playing time; and when he had time to throw, he had machine-like precision. And the supporting cast, particularly Davis, would provide a buffer for him and ease the pressure he would face.

On paper, it seemed like a perfect plan. In reality, it was something different. A 38-21 season-opening loss on *Monday Night Football* sounded alarms, and a two-game road trip to Kansas City and Tampa Bay kept the Broncos skidding. With future Hall of Famers like Derrick Thomas, Warren Sapp, and Derrick Brooks starting down Griese in Weeks 2 and 3, the young quarterback struggled and the problems multiplied from there.

Finally, in Week 4, the bottom fell out. With two minutes left in the first quarter, Griese was intercepted by Jets safety Victor Green and Terrell Davis tried to tackle him after a 15-yard return. In doing so, he shredded his right knee. Two ligaments—the anterior cruciate and medial collateral—were torn. The Broncos were 0-4 and compared with the team that won Super Bowl XXXIII, had lost the league MVP and the Super Bowl MVP. Linebacker John Mobley, defensive end Alfred Williams, and tight end Shannon Sharpe also missed a majority of games.

In the middle of this doomed season, the Broncos flew to Seattle to face the suddenly ascendant Seahawks. After missing the postseason for ten consecutive seasons and finishing .500 or worse eight years in a row, owner Paul Allen was getting serious about building a winner. He threw a massive contract and full organizational control to lure Mike Holmgren from Green Bay; he invested heavily in free agents; and he had a new stadium set to break ground in 2000. The Seahawks capitalized off the Broncos' slow start and stormed to the AFC West lead by October.

A month later, the 3-6 Broncos limped into the Kingdome for the final time before its implosion on March 26, 2000. In the 1970s and 1980s, the concrete hulk was one of the league's most raucous and formidable fortresses; the Broncos had one of their worst playoff defeats there, a 31-7 crumbling on Christmas Eve, 1983. But as the Seahawks declined under Ken Behring's shaky ownership in the 1990s, ticket sales declined. When the Broncos visited, their fans would gobble up thousands of seats, similar to what happens in the 2010s for games at Dallas, San Diego, and Minnesota.

The Seahawks' renaissance under Holmgren changed that. Their fans were charged, smelling the two-time defending champions' blood. And after the Broncos scored 17 points to take a third-quarter lead, Seattle rallied with 10 unanswered points in the fourth quarter. Veteran quarterback Chris Miller, filling in for an injured Griese, struggled to call the signals. The noise was as loud as Mile High Stadium in its heyday—enough to make your pant cuffs vibrate. Seattle held on for a 20-17 win that felt like the end of an era.

Shanahan's press conference lasted less than ninety seconds. He wanted to get the hell out of the Kingdome—and perhaps on to the next season as well. Although the Broncos played better and with enthusiasm down the stretch, their season was done at 3-7. They limped home with their worst finish in nine years, going 6-10 and facing mounting questions about Davis' knee, an aging defense, and whether Griese could handle the pressure involved with succeeding Elway.

CHAPTER FIVE

The 2000s

As the millennium dawned, the Broncos had to guard against a sense of satisfaction over their recent accomplishments.

There were the two world championships in 1997. There was the drive to approve taxpayer funding for a new stadium, which passed in 1998. That allowed shovels to go in the ground a few months later. By 2000, the new stadium—then dubbed "New Mile High," since it didn't yet have a corporate name on it—was rising where McNichols Sports Arena once stood, with the NBA Nuggets and NHL Avalanche having moved on the other side of Interstate 25 to the Pepsi Center.

In the front office, Shanahan remained firmly in charge. General manager Neal Dahlen, who arrived with Shanahan in 1995, assumed a lesser role in 2002 and was replaced by Ted Sundquist, a diligent former U.S. Air Force officer and world-class bobsledder who ascended through the ranks of the Broncos' scouting department. But Sundquist, like Dahlen, reported to Shanahan. This was a comfortable structure for the Broncos; most coaches since Lou Saban had final-say authority. But the sport was growing bigger and more complex, and the Broncos would find that replacing the greatest player in club history would not be easy. It would be so difficult, in fact, that the shadow of John Elway would linger. It didn't matter that Elway took many steps to cede the spotlight to the new generation of Broncos—staying away from Dove Valley and focusing on his business interests and an Arena Football League team, the Crush, that he began running in 2003.

To many fans, Elway still was the Broncos. The inevitable comparisons lobbed at his successors made the job description of "Broncos quarterback" one of the most difficult imaginable.

GRIESE LIGHTNING

B ut in 2000, Brian Griese looked like the man for the job. For a second consecutive season, he dealt with injuries; he missed seven games, including the Broncos' wild-card playoff loss at Baltimore on New Year's Eve. But when he played, he vacillated between steady and spectacular. The Broncos went 7-3 with Griese as the starter, and he earned a trip to the Pro Bowl, but a shoulder injury kept him out of the postseason.

Griese was healthier in 2001, but the Broncos were not. In the regular-season opener—which was also the first game at Invesco Field at Mile High—McCaffrey fractured his leg and was lost for the season. His injury was quickly forgotten by most who attended that game; about eight and a half hours after the Broncos wrapped up the 31-20 win over the New York Giants, the first of two jets hit the World Trade Center in New York City.

After a one-week pause to mourn following the 9/11 attacks, the Broncos resumed without McCaffrey and endured one of their more inconsistent seasons to date. After a 2-0 start, the Broncos would not win consecutive games until the next season. The final ten games were a perfect exchange of win, loss, win, loss, and despite a career season from wide receiver Rod Smith—113 catches, 1,343 yards and 11 touchdowns—the Broncos finished 8-8. Griese's interception ratio spiked from one every 84 attempts in 2000 to one every 23.7 attempts in 2001, and as the 2002 season began, his seat was warming.

The return of tight end Shannon Sharpe from a two-year stint in Baltimore and McCaffrey from injury helped. Both were productive and Sharpe had the best game of his career in a Week 6 win over the Kansas City Chiefs: 12 catches, 214 yards, and two touchdowns in a thrilling, 37-34 overtime win. But both were complements to Rod Smith, who was the clear No. 1 receiver. Both played two more seasons before retiring, and eventually both found careers in broadcasting: Sharpe with CBS Sports and then FOX Sports, and McCaffrey as the color analyst on the Broncos' radio broadcasts.

But Griese's ups and downs continued. Questions were raised about his consistency and leadership. Nevertheless, when the Broncos went to Oakland for a Week 16 showdown, they had a playoff spot in their sights; with wins in the final two games, they would win their first division title since 1998. Four days before kickoff, Griese called the game the biggest of his career. He didn't make it out of the second quarter, reinjuring his knee after throwing a pair of interceptions. Steve Beuerlein rallied the Broncos to within five points, but they fell 28-16. Three days later, Griese was benched. He was cut the following off-season and the Broncos would start over again at quarterback.

T.D.'s Last Run

By the 2002 preseason, knee problems finally felled Terrell Davis. He ran onto the field for a preseason game to get one last curtain call, then went to injured reserve. He basked in the adulation of appreciative fans, all of whom seemed a bit stunned at the relentless run of injuries that prematurely ended Davis' career.

His career numbers might pale when compared to others because of his injuries, but his four-season peak from 1995-98 includes crucial items that are missing from the résumés of most running backs: a league MVP award, a Super Bowl MVP, and a 2,000-yard season. In 2017, Davis was finally elected to the Hall of Fame.

"I think Tommy Nalen told me one time, 'He makes up for a multitude of sins that we would commit up front,' because there were a lot of times where there was nothing," said guard Brain Habib, a starter in the Broncos' Super Bowl XXXII win. "You'd watch the tape and on the front side of a play there might not be anything and he'd still make yardage."

Snake Charmed

Jake Plummer was well-known in Phoenix. After quarterbacking the Arizona State Sun Devils to their first Rose Bowl trip in a decade, the Cardinals made the local hero their second round pick in the subsequent 1997 NFL Draft and he became their starter at midseason. A year later, he led the Cardinals to their first playoff appearance since moving from St. Louis, and their first postseason win in a half-century, when they were still the Chicago Cardinals. Plummer was the face of a franchise that hadn't really had one for its first eight years in the desert.

But what he found as he got to know Denver was something different. His first glimpse was on December 29, 2002. It was the regular-season finale. Led by Beuerlein, who replaced the benched Griese, the Broncos rolled, 37-7. But the affable Beuerlein would turn thirty-eight just over two months later; at best, he was a temp at the position. Broncos fans at Invesco Field knew that Plummer was likely to be the hottest free-agent quarterback on the market, so some chanted, "We want Jake!"

"I was thinking in my head, 'I want you,'" Plummer would later recall.

Plummer had three choices when he hit free agency for the first time: Arizona, Chicago, and Denver. The first offered the comforts of familiarity with the offense, receivers, and the city. The second offered the most money but a dearth of offensive talent. In both cases, the head coach would be fired after the season.

Then there was Denver. Although Chicago had the more recent playoff appearance of the group, in 2001, that 13-3 finish was a fluke created by opportunistic defense and special teams. Those Bears went 8-0 in games decided by a touchdown or less. After a 4-12 season in 2002, that wasn't happening again, not without a rebuild.

The Broncos, on the other hand, were ready, even though they'd missed the playoffs two years in a row. Recent Pro Bowlers dotted the roster. Clinton Portis had just won NFL Offensive Rookie of the Year honors.

"You know where I've been, you know where my career has gone, and when it came down to the decision, it was all about winning," Plummer said.

Winning is exactly what he did. The Broncos went 40-18 in his starts. He set a Broncos passing yardage record in 2004, breaking John Elway's career high from 1993. (It has since been surpassed by Jay Cutler and Peyton Manning.) But Plummer also threw 20 interceptions that year, most coming in comeback situations, so a year later, he was recast by observers as "No-Mistake Jake," with less yardage and touchdowns but barely one-third as many picks, which gave him the opportunity to play in the Pro Bowl.

But Plummer was more than that. Completely at ease with himself, he took the stereotypes associated with big-time NFL stars, attached a stick of dynamite and pressed the button. His ride of choice for part of his time with the Broncos was an unassuming Honda Element. He grew out his beard and his hair, looking more like a hiker halfway into trekking down the Appalachian Trail than an NFL superstar. He wore Blu-Blocker sunglasses and brandished a 1970s moustache for a national-television interview.

But those were the superficial aspects. Plummer's personality went deeper. He was tireless in raising money for Alzheimer's Disease research. He was one of the most popular players ever to walk through the Broncos' locker room; his leadership a mix of cool confidence and a mellow, don't-sweat-the-small-stuff vibe. Friendship, like the bond he shared with Arizona State and Cardinals teammate Pat Tillman, mattered, much more than a trivial detail of a 300-page game plan that was unlikely to see the light of game day anyway. Tillman left football in 2002 to join the Army following the 9/11 attacks, and was killed in Afghanistan in 2004.

"When I got (to the NFL), you realize it's still just football and sometimes it can be way too serious," Plummer said.

"I loved Jake. Fun, fun guy to play with, man," center Tom Nalen would recall in 2013. "In the huddle, just loose and just kind of not your prototypical quarterback."

"As far as joking around goes, I've got to stay loose," Plummer said. "If I'm tight and nervous and not being myself, the guys will feel that, the guys will see that. I'm not a jokester that's going around playing practical jokes. I'm myself."

But pundits usually did not see that.

A left-handed toss out of the end zone in the 2004 season opener against the Chiefs was to be at the top of any litany of issues that critics recited regarding Plummer. But that was part of being an improvisational artist as he could be. Not every meander away from the playbook is going to be successful. But most were. His teammates respected and adored him for it. This was an organic, vibrant way to play; it wasn't mechanical or constructed. Both styles can work, but it's up to the quarterback to be true to what fits him best.

Plummer was born to freelance. Unfortunately for him, he was in an offensive scheme that frowned on it. Shanahan wanted to channel that innate feel for the game into a system; he saw the potential for greatness. But it didn't mesh. It was like trying to put a stallion in a stable. He can linger there for a while, but eventually he has to get out and gallop or he's not true to the essence of his being.

In other sports, we celebrate creativity: the dazzling passes of Steve Nash; the improvisational, preternatural feel of Lionel Messi; the aerial acrobatics of Olympic gold medalist Shaun White. But in football, we tend to venerate playing by the numbers, perhaps more than is necessary. Just because Peyton Manning is justifiably admired for his precision and perfectionism doesn't mean we can't also celebrate a Plummer. Some quarterbacks are conductors. Others are the lead singers of jam bands. But done well, it can all be art.

In reflecting on the Plummer era, it's the organic, unpredictable artistry that I remember. The play-action rollout and deep pass through the snowfall to Rod Smith. The quick twitch of his body to elude a defender and get the pass away. Even the quick middle finger to jeering fans in the stands that he delivered on December 12, 2004, during a win over Miami; that was the kind of response I wanted to give to message-board knuckleheads who criticized my writing, my intelligence, and my manhood.

But more than all that, I recall Plummer's knowledge that some things were bigger than football. That paying tribute to a close friend like Tillman was worth drawing the league's ire because you wanted to keep the memorial decal on your helmet for longer than was mandated. Plummer was right about more aspects of football and life than I would have believed years ago; the passage of time continues to illuminate his wisdom. His teammates recall him fondly, and from my perch in the press box, so do I.

"It wasn't 100 percent football, which I think you actually need that—100 percent football can be dangerous," Nalen said. "Jake was awesome, left-handed passes and all."

THE MOMENT THAT CHANGES YOUR LIFE

Personnel executives and coaches have some painful duties—none more so than cutting a player. But at the opposite end of the emotional spectrum are the phone calls they make to their draft picks. Even for a seventh-round selection, it's a dramatic, destiny-altering moment.

In 2003, the Broncos caused a bit of a surprise by taking Georgia offensive tackle George Foster with their first-round pick. Foster was raw and had been a backup for most of his senior season following an automobile accident, but the Broncos had decided to gamble on Foster's quick feet, athleticism, and potential.

Foster knew the call would come from some NFL team—but not necessarily in the first round.

"I remember talking to (general manager) Ted Sundquist and asking, 'Are you sure? Are you for real?' He was like, 'Yeah.' I was like, 'Nah, quit playing,'" Foster recalled. "You hear stories about people getting calls and then the team never drafts them and that call doesn't really mean anything, so I was kind of skeptical."

Although Foster had his doubts, the draft party raged. The family home became a social center. Every room was filled with family, friends, well-wishers—even members of his family's church.

"I was in the den, watching the television. You had people outside, in different rooms, all over," Foster said. "We had set one of our TVs out on the porch—a little 20-inch TV, set out on a table in the yard. The reaction was resounding around the house, but everybody wasn't in the same room.

"It ended up being a very joyous occasion."

A year earlier, tight end Jeb Putzier watched the draft with skepticism. If the Boise State tight end was going to be selected, it wouldn't happen until the later rounds, by which time only die-hards and draftniks usually have any interest.

But every prospect, even late-round ones, has to deal with the questions from people in his midst. To them, a potential NFL player in the family or social circle is an extraordinary circumstance. Reality may dictate a low pick or a spot outside the draft, but as Putzier learned, people he knew thought he was a sure thing.

"Everybody was bugging me," Putzier said. "I didn't think I was going to get drafted; I didn't think I had a chance."

So instead of dealing with the queries, he threw everyone out.

"I made everyone leave the house," Putzier said. "My brother and I played PlayStation on one TV while we watched the draft on the other one. I talked to numerous teams that day."

And that's another part of the draft—the calls. You wait for the one that says, "Welcome." But before that, you deal with the teams saying, "If you're on the board, we'll pick you," only to follow another path. There's more misdirection than in the pre-snap motion of the Don Coryell offense, circa 1980.

"Kansas City called me at 5:30 in the morning," Putzier recalled with bemusement. "I was like, 'Thanks.'"

The Broncos called him later that afternoon, and he'd remain there for the next four years.

"They were the last team I thought would draft me. It was all really random," he said.

Still, his experience was better than others. His fellow 2002 rookie, Lenny Walls, would end up as a starting cornerback for the Broncos. But he wasn't drafted at all—much to his dismay.

"Draft day was gruesome for me. I expected to go on the first day," Walls remembered. "The hardest part was my mom expecting me to get drafted and not getting drafted."

But there can be advantages to going undrafted: if multiple teams call, you can weigh offers against each other, and take the best deal—whether it happens to be financial or for playing time.

"Mike Shanahan was a convincing person," Walls said. "(After a conversation) I was ready to go play for him."

The Rise of the Internet

The dot-com era changed how teams were covered and the evolution of football media continues to this day. By the early 2000s, all teams had their own websites, with staff members covering the team like newspapers had for so long, albeit usually with a team-supporting slant.

In 2002, the Broncos brought me to Denver to handle this part of their operation, joining veteran staffer Mike Sarro. The only problem with it was that the sites weren't yet large enough in scope to justify having a proper staff. Thus, in addition to writing stories, I produced video reports, shot photographs when the need arose, and had to help handle tasks for the marketing department. It was multi-tasking to the extreme. But the culture of the organization demanded it; the Dove Valley office was not—and is not—a haven for slackers.

In those days, teams and league sites alike tried to get players to conduct live, on-line chats or question-and-answer sessions. Some of the better admissions never saw the light of day, like the beefy 300-pound lineman—who shall remain nameless—who admitted that he listened to Celine Dion music before games to get pumped up. But others were more forthcoming. Backup quarterback Steve Beuerlein admitted in a fan question-and-answer session that he listened to *Let the Good Times Roll* by The Cars and *Right Now* by Van Halen before every game. Tight end Wesley Duke was willing to post a picture of himself riding an elephant when he was allocated to NFL Europe.

Other players took it a step further—or, in the case of Nate Jackson, several miles of steps. In six years as a Bronco, he was promoted from the practice squad to the 53-man roster, changed positions, spent a spring in NFL Europe, and endured numerous injuries. The constant of those years was a journal on the team website that was usually the most creative content of the hundreds of thousands of words published on an annual basis. He honed his craft and by 2013 published a revealing and critically acclaimed memoir of his life in the NFL. Another player who found his voice through the site was cornerback Domonique Foxworth, who also wrote an illuminating series of blog entries before being traded to the Atlanta Falcons in 2008. Foxworth became a key figure in the NFL Players' Association after having his playing career cut short by knee injuries and is now COO of the National Basketball Players Association.

What players like these possess is natural intelligence, a willingness to examine themselves and their football life, and a desire to share this experience and help others understand the game and the player from the inside.

Rod Smith: Doing It the Right Way

There are no "Employee of the Month" plaques displayed anywhere at Broncos headquarters. If there were, they would have been useless, because for more than a decade, the only name displayed would have been Rod Smith's.

Other companies have plaques with pictures, honoring their Employees of the Month. For the most dutiful of corporate servants, there are repeated spots on the plaques over the years, enough to where you can watch that employee's hairline recede.

Smith played fourteen seasons. Not thirteen. This is crucial. The NFL record books say that Smith accrued thirteen seasons of service time, from 1995 to 2007, with his last year spent on injured reserve. But in 1994, he was on the practice squad as a rookie. Just because he didn't travel with the team to road games and wear a uniform on Sundays did not mean Smith was any less diligent.

His experience on the practice squad helped make him the leader he would become. In the locker room, he would offer advice on pass-catching, financial planning, weight training, or an opinion on any subject you could imagine. The last receiver on the practice squad mattered just as much to him as Ed McCaffrey. He knew from experience how hard they worked.

Smith also had a memory like an elephant's. Even in 2012, eighteen years after he broke into the league, he tweeted, "Did I get drafted yet? I'm still waiting." That chip stayed on his shoulder his entire career, and based on that tweet, it remains there today.

You could trust Smith because he had a sharp edge to him. When I see nothing but a smooth, polished demeanor, I find myself questioning that person's motives; once I see the razor come out—be it in frustration, anger, exasperation—I know that's someone I can trust.

You'd see it from Smith when he received a question that irked him—or occasionally when you'd ask him for a minute and he'd quickly, forcefully decline. But invariably, a second or two later, he'd look back at you and ask, "What do you want?" Then he'd pour his heart, soul, and guts into your tape recorder.

You can call Smith the Broncos' all-time leading receiver, the league's leader in receptions and receiving yards among undrafted players, a Hall of Fame candidate, or a Ring of Fame inductee. Just don't call Smith an "overachiever," which was the word most often applied to him during his playing days. He hated that.

"What makes you an overachiever? I never understood that word—overachiever. That means you're doing something you're not supposed to be able to do, because obviously we were able to do it. It's just a matter of having the right opportunities," he said.

"You don't know when you're going to get them, so you've got to be prepared for them at all times. You never know when this game is going to end, so you've got to go like it's your last day. And that's the way I've approached it. Every day I come in here, I look to make sure that my name is in my locker. That means I've got another day."

He could overcome being undrafted. He could overcome the critiques that he was too small and too slow to achieve NFL success. The only thing he couldn't overcome was a balky hip that began bothering him in 2004 and hastened the end of his career.

"Honestly, I (played) for a while without knowing it was probably doing more damage than good to (the hip)," Smith said. "My mentality is what kept me here this long, being able to withstand pain and play hurt, but when you get injured, it's a different thing. That same tenacity that helped me stay in the league this long is probably going to take me out of the league."

When Smith retired, he resisted overtures to coach. There was too much else to do: businesses to run, family that needed his presence.

And he didn't want to keep coaches' hours. That was all right. In every way, Rod Smith gave at the office. And to this day, he still pops up at Dove Valley to offer counsel, and still shows up at games to help rouse the fans and his successors in orange and blue.

To me, he is the quintessential Bronco. Devoted, diligent, and a man who acknowledges his imperfections and works as hard at overcoming them as he did in becoming the player he was. To this day, the organization is stronger when he walks through the front doors.

So Close, But So Far

After three seasons as a backup quarterback, Jarious Jackson did not survive the final cut to fifty-three players in 2003. But that wasn't the end and after injuries shelved Jake Plummer and Steve Beuerlein in October, the Broncos re-signed Jackson, since they desperately needed a quarterback who knew the offense.

It was a moment for which he'd prepared when he was off the roster. After two weeks "sitting on my butt," Jackson realized that if he ever wanted to play again, he needed to take action.

Over the next five weeks, Jackson and three other preseason casualties—wide receiver Herb Haygood, running back Marlion Jackson, and wide receiver Darcey Levy—would gather at the youth soccer fields on the other side of the intersection of Broncos Parkway and Potomac Street, where Dove Valley sat.

From a few hundred yards away, they could hear their teammates practicing, coaches' whistles blowing, and the blasts of the air horn: once to signify the end of a practice period, twice to end the entire day's on-field. So the quartet of ex-Broncos went through exactly what they would do if they were still on the roster—at least, as much as they could do with only four men.

"We'd just go out there and throw; we'd hear the horns blowing and the whole nine (yards)," Jackson said. "When they switched periods, we switched periods."

It didn't assure Jackson of a long-term stay in Denver; after he struggled in a starting assignment during a meaningless regular-season finale at Green Bay, he was converted to defense in the following off-season, then released. But the experience did help Jackson play again and he enjoyed an eight-year career playing quarterback in the Canadian Football League, where he is now a coach.

LET'S MAKE A DEAL

The genesis of the biggest trade in recent Broncos history was a conversation in the bleachers at a practice in Mobile, Alabama.

That was where Jack Reale, the agent for cornerback Champ Bailey, walked up to general manager Ted Sundquist and expressed the possibility that the perennial Pro Bowl cornerback, then coming off his fifth season and fourth Pro Bowl selection, would be given permission to seek a trade.

Sundquist and Reale had a prior business relationship. In the previous year, they hammered out contracts for starting safety Nick Ferguson and long-time kicker Jason Elam, with Elam signing a five-year contract that kept him in Denver through 2007, his fifteenth season.

After the Indianapolis Colts had shredded Denver's secondary in a 41-10 wild-card pounding on January 4, 2004, Sundquist and Mike Shanahan knew they needed to upgrade their secondary. It wasn't for a lack of trying; the team's first-round picks in 2000 and 2001, Deltha O'Neal and Willie Middlebrooks, were both cornerbacks. But O'Neal was benched at midseason of 2003 and eventually tried at receiver, and Middlebrooks never became more than a spot player on defense and a decent special-teamer. By the postseason loss at Indianapolis, the Broncos started undrafted Lenny Walls and Kelly Herndon. That a pair of young cornerbacks had come from outside the draft was testament to the Broncos' thorough scouting but it was anything but ideal. Denver needed a lockdown cornerback, which the team had not had since Ring of Famer Louis Wright patrolled the secondary.

Enter Bailey, who watched the Colts' thorough decimation of Denver's defense.

"It was a rough game to watch," Bailey said when he joined the Broncos. "I don't see that happening much more, and I definitely want to help put an end to games like that."

But to get something, you've got to give up something. That became running back Clinton Portis, the NFL's offensive rookie of the year in 2002. Portis had quickly become beloved in Denver; he was colorful and dressed in wild clothes, but he was also dominant, brash, and wanted a new contract well before his rookie deal was up.

"With where we were at with Clinton, everything that we were hearing—that I was hearing—was that there was the possibility of a hold-out," Sundquist said. "Every indication that I was being given from that side was that there was a definite possibility that there would be a holdout.

"You want a happy player. You don't want the distraction there, and we're trying to win championships. We're not trying to just exist. And those are distractions. At that point, Coach Shanahan felt like the best thing was to say, 'Hey, if you can go out and find the deal that you're looking for and you can get us the compensation that we feel is fair, then we'll let you do that.'"

Portis found it with the Redskins, who had just rehired Hall of Fame head coach Joe Gibbs after he spent eleven years tending to his NASCAR team. Gibbs had bellwether running backs during his first D.C. administration—John Riggins, George Rogers, Earnest Byner—and wanted another, but wanted one who was younger.

"They went to Washington, and at that point Washington really wasn't interested in giving up the draft choices we were wanting," Sundquist said. "But they knew they had Champ, and that he was not happy there. Obviously, our quest for a shutdown corner is well-documented."

And with that, Reale called Sundquist and the wheels were set in motion for a mammoth deal that would be a high point of the decade. It was the first swap of Pro Bowlers from the previous season since a 1973 John Hadl-for-Coy Bacon deal between the Los Angeles Rams and San Diego Chargers. It was arguably the Broncos' biggest trade involving a veteran player since the Craig Morton-for-Steve Ramsey deal in 1977, and perhaps their most important exchange of any kind since the John Elway trade of 1983. Washington threw in a second-round pick to sweeten the deal, and it was consummated.

It was the rare trade that pleased both sides. Portis was effective and often dominant in Washington. But like many running backs, the collection of hits caused attrition and he carried the football for the last time in 2010. Bailey, meanwhile, would go to three more Pro Bowls after that. Portis finished his career just 77 yards shy of hitting 10,000. Bailey was with the Broncos through 2013 and retired after being released by the Saints on the eve of the 2014 season. It will be an upset if he is not a first-ballot Hall of Famer, and his Ring of Fame place seems equally assured.

"I want to be the best ever, and I don't think I'm anywhere near that right now," Bailey said on his first day in Denver.

Whether Bailey is the best ever will be a matter for historians to debate. But at minimum, the conversation about the best cornerback in league history must include Bailey. His 2005-06 apex was arguably the best any cornerback has played in league history. Even as he aged, he continued launching one Pro Bowl season after another, and didn't lose his lockdown status until 2013, when age and a nagging foot injury suffered in the preseason finally caught up to him in his sixteenth NFL season and his tenth as a Bronco.

Just as crucial to the success of the deal was that the Broncos were able to replace Portis for a few years with a stable of running backs whose members changed annually. In 2004, 2005, and 2006, the Broncos got 1,000-yard seasons out of Reuben Droughns, Mike Anderson, and Tatum Bell, respectively. Bell was the player who the Broncos drafted with the second-round pick they got from Washington. Only in 2007 and 2008 did the Broncos' reservoir of 1,000-yard running backs run dry.

But Bailey was around long enough to see the Broncos' running game return to form when Willis McGahee and Knowshon Moreno launched 1,000-yard seasons in 2011 and 2013. In 2011, the Broncos' running game was the league's best. Meanwhile, Bailey kept doing what he did for so long, going one-on-one against a foe's top wide receiver and shutting him down.

THE LEGACY OF SAFETIES CONTINUES

Goose Gonsoulin. Billy Thompson. Steve Foley. Dennis Smith. Steve Atwater. These were just the biggest names in the Broncos' glorious history at safety during their first four decades. John Lynch fit right in after signing with the Broncos in 2004 after he was cut by the Tampa Bay Buccaneers.

When the Bucs released Lynch, the prevailing thought was that he was in decline. But Lynch would play in four Pro Bowls in four Broncos seasons. He might not have had the same speed as he did during his younger days with Tampa Bay, but his penchant for punishing hits remained and his anticipation was better.

Along with Bailey, Lynch revitalized the Broncos secondary. Before injuries caught up to Lynch in 2007, his final season, Bailey and Lynch helped the Broncos defense give up just 18.1 points per game from 2004-06—3.8 fewer than the defense allowed in the previous three seasons.

Lynch will be remembered more for his Bucs years, and since he won a Super Bowl there, that's understandable. But like Gary Zimmerman in the 1990s, he still had plenty left at the end of his career, and delivered toughness, accountability, and leadership.

When Jerry Rice Wore Orange and Blue

In the early 2000s, Mike Shanahan had a fetish for signing grizzled veteran receivers in an attempt to wring one final wisp of greatness from them before they retired. Pro Football Hall of Famer Andre Reed, ex-Pro Bowler Rob Moore, and former Brett Favre target Robert Brooks were among the proven veterans who tried –and failed—to contribute to the Broncos. Usually they lost out to young receivers who would end up having a fraction of their career impact but who had the speed the old hands lacked.

But none of these caught as much attention as Jerry Rice, who signed with the Broncos in May 2005. Rice owned three Super Bowl rings and a slew of league records. He had nothing to prove. Yet he rejoined Shanahan, his offensive coordinator in San Francisco from 1993-94, for one final attempt at extending his career.

While he was the center of attention on the practice field, the city of Denver let Rice be. One night not long after arriving, he had dinner in a prominent local steakhouse. He sat at the bar undisturbed as he ate, not an autograph hound to be found. He was left to focus on his task at hand that night and throughout the summer of 2005.

But nothing about Rice in a Broncos uniform seemed right. His customary No. 80 belonged to Rod Smith, the franchise's standard-bearer at wide receiver, so Rice instead wore No. 19. The orange swooshes on the side of the uniform looked out of place on Rice. The meticulous effort and precision in his routes was there, but Rice's forty-two-year-old body lacked the speed to gain adequate separation, and the league's most decorated receiver looked slow and shockingly ordinary.

By the end of the preseason, Rice had earned a spot on the Broncos' 53-man roster. But as the No. 4 receiver, he was likely to be inactive most games, as he only had a backup position and would not contribute on special teams. This wasn't the 2010s, which is the epoch of four-receiver sets; this was 2005, when the Broncos used a fullback extensively and rarely lined up with more than three wide receivers. Rice was given two choices: accept this role or retire.

He chose the latter, and thus his Hall of Fame plaque does not include the words "Denver Broncos," since he was never on the roster for a regular-season game. But despite that, his presence is remembered for the glimpse of greatness he offered his teammates.

"We shared a little bit in that," said Smith. "Even though there wasn't a regular-season catch or anything like that, we shared a little bit in that."

Nearly a decade later, you still occasionally see a "RICE 19" jersey around Denver. He didn't have a catch as a Bronco, but he reminded everyone in the organization of what it meant to be a professional. That pales compared with his legacy in San Francisco or even Oakland, but it mattered, even if it goes down as nothing more than a footnote to the career of the greatest wide receiver to play the sport.

NOT EVERY GAMBLE PAYS OFF

The first day of the 2005 NFL Draft was ending. The final pick belonged to the Broncos; it was a compensatory selection issued to them based on their losses in the previous year's free-agent class—most prominently starting linebacker Ian Gold and double-digit sacker Bertrand Berry.

No one knew the Broncos were about to steal the spotlight from No. 1 overall pick Alex Smith, who had gone to the 49ers over ten hours earlier. But when the Broncos turned in the draft card with the name, "Maurice Clarett," the dominant team of the day was one that didn't even have a first-round pick. More than a few expletives flew in the media room as stories were rewritten and television packages re-edited.

The Broncos had taken the single most polarizing player in the draft. He had not played in a game for twenty-seven months, having been embroiled in one eligibility fight after another. The most recent glimpse of him came at a disastrous Scouting Combine workout two months earlier; in that session, he'd run the 40-yard dash in 4.72 and 4.82 seconds, then quit. These led to pointed questions for which Shanahan needed more than an immediate answer but a defensible rationalization.

"That could be a misconception," Shanahan said. "How do you know that he had speed at Ohio State when he ran as a freshman? Terrell Davis wasn't, so called, very fast. But he played very fast in games and had great cutting ability. So speed isn't always a factor."

Still, it was what everyone wanted to talk about. And it was why Clarett figured he would be sitting at home the next day, waiting for a team to call.

"I had actually turned the TV off and had got in the car," Clarett said.

Barely fifteen hours later, he was at Dove Valley, touring the facility with fellow first-day picks Darrent Williams, Domonique Foxworth, and Karl Paymah. Clarett was the only one of the group who was not a cornerback. He said the right things as he met the media. Shanahan talked him up by citing the Broncos' track record; a year earlier, Reuben Droughns had become the fifth different running back in the past seven seasons to break 1,000 yards in orange and blue. Clarett seemed poised to be the sixth.

"We feel like we know running backs pretty good," Shanahan said. "We've had some success with them. We think he'll fit into our system very well. Now only time will tell if he takes advantage of the situation."

It didn't take much time to reveal that he would not. Clarett clashed with media. He was out of shape, which led to nagging injuries. The explosion and balance he displayed in leading Ohio State to the national championship as a freshman three years earlier was gone, and he slipped down the depth chart. Nevertheless, he continued to draw attention. Between Clarett trying to start his career and Rice trying to delay retirement for one more year after twenty seasons, the 2005 camp became a bit of a circus.

But Rice was at least taking meaningful repetitions, played extensively in the preseason, and was serving as model for others to emulate. None of that applied to Clarett, who was so buried that he did not even play a snap in the preseason.

The only positive for the Broncos was that the roll of the dice didn't affect their budget or salary cap. Because Clarett signed a heavily incentive-based contract that had no guaranteed money, the Broncos cut him with no "dead money" remaining against the salary cap.

Clarett never sniffed the NFL again, but after getting his life together while incarcerated, he reunited with Ted Sundquist in 2010 for a season with the Omaha Nighthawks of the short-lived United Football League. A small colony of ex-Broncos followed Sundquist to Omaha, including tight end Jeb Putzier, offensive linemen P.J. Alexander and

George Foster, defensive tackle Demetrin Veal, linebacker Nick Greisen, and assistant coach Kirk Doll. But none attracted more attention than Clarett, whose efforts to reassemble the pieces of his life and counsel others to avoid his mistakes appear to have been successful.

EAT FRESH, PLAY FRESH

On the fringes of the NFL, players will do almost anything to keep the dream of playing on Sundays alive. And usually, the jobs they must take are the kind that can be worked at odd hours and have a quick and painless severance, because days must be reserved for staying in football shape and the call from an NFL team can come at any time.

For wide receiver David Kircus, that meant spending the 2005 season working at a Subway in Michigan after being released by the Detroit Lions.

"I did it in high school too, so I had a little experience—not that I needed much," Kircus said. "'They paid me pretty well to do it, it was fun. It was free food."

During the 2006 off-season, I wrote about Kircus, as I did for many unheralded players trying to stick on the roster. Of course, this story went viral—at least, what qualified for "viral" in the days when Facebook was mostly used by college students and Twitter was only in its prototype stage. It became fodder for locker-room and on-field jokes and defensive backs would frequently reference his "Sandwich Artist" days when taunting him in one-on-one drills.

Despite the teasing, Kircus stuck on the 53-man roster for a season, beating out a second-round pick from two years earlier (Darius Watts) and a former first-round pick of the Chicago Bears (David Terrell) in the process.

Jason Elam, World Traveler

No Bronco scored more points or drilled more game-winning kicks than Jason Elam. In the 2007 season alone, Elam's field goals were responsible for four walk-off wins; without him, that modest 7-9 season might have been a disaster.

But no Bronco had a bigger world than Elam, who grew up in the South, went all the way to Hawai'I for college and ended up relocating to Alaska following his retirement from the game.

Elam is a devout evangelical Christian so he's the last person you would expect to see in a darkened corner of a bar with a Mexican beer in his hand and multiple women at his side. But in some ways, Elam is the real-life version of the "Most Interesting Man in the World"—or at least, the "Most Interesting Man to Wear a Broncos Uniform."

He's written multiple novels. He's a seasoned pilot who once aspired to work for an airline but now makes his living flying around Alaska. He's hopscotched around the globe, often on mission trips. His travelogue includes Kenya, South Africa, Turkey, Uganda, and Israel. During his playing career, he would load an airplane with food, plants, and flowers and fly to remote corners of Alaska.

Elam and his family fell in love with the forty-ninth state and settled there after his career ended in the 2009 season when the Atlanta Falcons cut him after his accuracy and distance suddenly vanished at midseason. He signed a one-day contract the following spring and retired as he deserved to: as a Bronco.

A Dynasty Dethroned

The seeding and records said the Broncos should have been favored over the New England Patriots when they collided in the divisional playoffs on a balmy 54-degree night. The only problem was that the Patriots had won nine consecutive playoff games under Bill Belichick, were the reigning back-to-back world champions, and had won three of the previous four Vince Lombardi trophies.

The Patriots were beset by injuries, but their aura of invincibility was at its zenith by the time their team plane landed in Denver on January 13, 2006. It was the Broncos' first home playoff game in seven years. The area was so abuzz that the Patriots' convoy of buses was followed by local news helicopters, broadcasting its journey along freeways as it navigated Friday night rush-hour traffic to the hotel.

The Broncos were up for the challenge—none more than Champ Bailey. With one minute left in the third quarter and the Patriots driving to a touchdown that would have put them in front 13-10, Bailey flipped the game, stepping in front of a Tom Brady pass for Troy Brown and sprinting 100 yards before being knocked out of bounds at the New England 1-yard-line.

With every step Bailey took, the crowd roared louder—especially toward the end when Bailey was running out of gas and laboring as the yards flew below his feet.

"I definitely thought I was there, but I really didn't have anything left," he said. "By the time I got to the 30 it was all willpower pushing me in the end zone then."

At the goal line, Patriots tight end Ben Watson sent him flying out of bounds. The ball flew out of his hand, leading the Patriots to protest that Bailey had fumbled the football out of the end zone for a touchback. But the challenge failed and the call stood—not that Bailey noticed.

"I was on the ground because I was gassed. I couldn't even get up and walk," he said.

Fortunately for the Broncos, Mike Anderson finished the job, running around the left side for a touchdown. The 14-point swing powered the Broncos to a 27-13 win. For the first time since the Elway era, the Broncos were postseason winners. Bailey got the game ball. But the joy wouldn't last long.

Be Careful What You Wish For ...

The next day, Broncos players weren't openly hoping to avoid an AFC Championship trip to Indianapolis, which would have sent them back to the place where their last two playoff trips ended in the wild-card round. But you could sense the excitement in Colorado when Colts kicker Mike Vanderjagt missed a last-gasp, game-tying field-goal attempt. The No. 6 seed Steelers moved on and the Broncos were set to host the AFC Championship.

"Pittsburgh came to us, and everybody was excited about that," recalled wide receiver Rod Smith, "and I was like, 'No. You've got to go play. It's not about being excited about playing at home. It has nothing to do with that. You've got a football game. You can't worry about all the other stuff.'

"Honestly, I saw a lot of our younger guys kind of got lost in the fact that we had a home game, instead of getting lost in the fact of getting in that playbook, being focused, being disciplined on the things that we need to do as a team."

Early in the game, opportunities for takeaways were lost. Eventually, Steelers quarterback Ben Roethlisberger began peppering the Broncos secondary with passes. Cornerback Darrent Williams was hurt and less effective than normal. And then, with the Steelers leading 17-3 and the Broncos needing to get to halftime and hit the reset button, Plummer tried to make a play—and instead threw a pass for Stephen Alexander that was intercepted.

It was 24-3 at halftime, and a second-half rally petered out in a 34-17 loss that was the Broncos' most lopsided home playoff defeat.

"We were so close and just picked a bad day for the whole team to have a bad day," Nalen recalled seven years later.

The entire trajectory of the franchise seemed to change that day. The next month, defensive lineman Trevor Pryce and running back Mike Anderson were cut after stellar seasons; both were casualties of the salary cap. Two months later, the Broncos traded up to select Vanderbilt quarterback Jay Cutler, effectively starting the countdown to when Plummer's time as starter would end.

It concluded after a Thanksgiving night loss at Kansas City. The Broncos were 7-4 and still in excellent position for a wild-card bid that would have been their fourth consecutive playoff appearance. But inconsistent offense led Shanahan to change quarterbacks, and he jettisoned Plummer for Cutler. The offense as a whole was struggling, particularly on the line, where veteran left tackle Matt Lepsis had been lost for the season to a torn anterior cruciate ligament. But as is so often the case, the quarterback took the blame, even though it was not a coincidence that the Broncos went 5-1 with Lepsis in the starting lineup that season and 4-6 without him.

The 2006 season was one of the most maddening in Broncos history. But within twelve hours of its end, it meant nothing.

"D-Will"

December 31, 2006, was like any other game day for Darrent Williams. The Broncos' second-round pick in 2005, Williams had established himself as a dynamic, tenacious cornerback playing opposite Champ Bailey, and was also an explosive punt returner. Between Williams and Domonique Foxworth, the Broncos had quality cornerbacks other than Bailey. Man-to-man coverage was a strength of the defense.

As was his custom, Williams asked teammates, "All ready?" He played with spirit and enthusiasm. It wasn't enough to give the Broncos a win; they lost in overtime, and the playoff bid that was in their grasp went to the Kansas City Chiefs by virtue of a tiebreaker.

Several hours later, none of that mattered. Williams had been shot while in the back of a limousine leaving a party. He died in the arms of teammate Javon Walker. At just twenty-four, Williams left behind a heartbroken family, a stunned city, and a shattered team.

It was the darkest hour in the history of the Broncos. The organization had only begun to pick up the pieces when tragedy struck again. Running back Damien Nash collapsed and died at his St. Louis, Missouri, home on February 24, 2007, just fifty-four days after Williams.

Tragedy is something every professional sports organization must deal with; life, and death, intrudes as it does anywhere else. But the loss of two vibrant young men within two months rocked the Broncos to their core; at times, it appeared too much to bear.

The club rallied around the families and close friends of both players, and paid tribute to both with a helmet decal. The Broncos also named the teen center at the Broncos Boys and Girls Club in the Montbello neighborhood of east Denver for Williams. Williams spent much of his childhood hanging out at a Boys and Girls Club in Fort Worth, Texas, and during his two years with the Broncos, volunteered at the Denver club. The legacy remains, and has only grown. But we all would rather have Nash and Williams still around than just the memories and scars.

"Toro! Toro!"

The clouds over the Broncos had not parted in the preseason. They traded for former Lions cornerback Dré Bly to replace Williams, but through no fault of Bly's own, the nine-year veteran couldn't bring the same energy and spirit that Williams did. Defensive lineman Ebenezer Ekuban was playing the best football of his career, but tore his right Achilles tendon in a preseason loss at Dallas.

The Broncos needed a jolt. They got it as the seconds ticked down to zero in the regular-season opener at Buffalo. Trailing 15-14, Javon Walker had just caught an 11-yard pass from Cutler to move the Broncos into field-goal range. But he fell down inbounds, and there were no timeouts remaining.

The clock drained. The Broncos had to exchange their eleven offensive players for the eleven needed for the field-goal team. They had a call they used to signal the change: "Toro! Toro!"

"You don't have time to think about it, you don't have time to worry about it; you don't have time to second-guess, you just have to keep your poise and play," said tight end Nate Jackson, who was part of the field-goal team. "We act on instinct. That's when we do best."

Not many Broncos could see the game clock. But Bills fans, giddy over a potential Week 1 upset, counted down the seconds.

"Buffalo fans, thanks to them, because they actually gave us the countdown on the time," safety Nick Ferguson said. "Guys knew exactly when to get down."

The snap flew back toward holder Todd Sauerbrun with one second left. He placed the ball down for Jason Elam, who drilled the 42-yard attempt, allowing the Broncos to snap a two-game Week 1 skid.

A week later, they won under equally interesting circumstances.

THE LAST-SECOND TIMEOUT

Full disclosure: I hate when teams call timeout a split-second before the football is snapped on a field-goal attempt. It's legal, but it's cynical. It's too much gamesmanship for my tastes. And after Mike Shanahan pulled the tactic out of his hat when the Oakland Raiders visited Invesco Field at Mile High on September 16, 2007, it went viral.

That's because it worked on Oakland kicker Sebastian Janikowski. Shanahan told an official that he was going to take a timeout just before the snap and had a plan for exactly when he wanted to call it.

"Well you want to get it down there when their kicker is focused and ready to kick," Shanahan explained. "You want to do it soon enough so you know he is looking for and adjusting and not looking back at the holder. When he started to look up is when I called it."

But with a sold-out crowd screaming to try and distract Janikowski, no one heard. Jon Condo snapped the football, and Janikowski sent the kick through the uprights. The Raiders celebrated; the Broncos dropped their heads.

Then came word that a timeout had been called. Janikowski had to reflect on the kick and ponder the pressure. Moments later, his second attempt slammed into the left upright. The Broncos capitalized, driving nine plays to Elam's game-winning 23-yard field goal.

The tactic doesn't always work. Five weeks later, Elam faced a potential game-winning 49-yard attempt against the Steelers. As the clock wound toward the attempt, the Steelers called timeout with two seconds left.

"Honestly, it helps," Elam said. "The field was pretty chewed up, so I was able to make sure that I had a good spot," he said. "(You can) see what the wind's doing and just you're able to collect yourself a little more. So I like it."

Elam's assertion did not stop coaches at all levels from making the last-split-second timeout a tool in their satchels. Of course, few kickers had the mental fortitude of Elam, which is how he endured for seventeen seasons in the NFL.

THE FALL OF AN EMPIRE

The Broncos' best player, John Elway, had the perfect send-off to his playing career. Just under a decade later, their winningest coach, Mike Shanahan, would not be so fortunate. Two days after the 2008 season concluded, Shanahan was fired by owner Pat Bowlen, ending a relationship between Shanahan and the Broncos that began when Dan Reeves hired him away from the University of Florida in 1984 to work as the Broncos' quarterbacks coach.

"I just felt that it was time for change," Bowlen explained a day after calling Shanahan into his office and firing him. "Twenty-one years of being at one organization and fourteen years as head coach is about long enough."

Partings in the NFL are rarely tinged with sweetness, and that was the case for Shanahan. Bowlen dismissed him after three consecutive seasons out of the playoffs and with a 17-20 record after replacing Jake Plummer at quarterback with Jay Cutler in December 2006. But despite the on-field struggles, Shanahan's sacking was a surprise to many inside and outside the Broncos organization. Bowlen had given him multiple contract extensions, and even declared Shanahan his "coach for life."

"Well, I've said that. But I don't have any regrets about saying it," Bowlen said. "I guess nothing is forever."

Toward the end of the Shanahan era, things got bizarre around Broncos, headquarters. In May 2007, he arranged for David Kircus, a backup wide receiver, to take a lie-detector test after he was arrested on a second-degree assault charge. Kircus later plead guilty to a misdemeanor assault charge and was eventually cut.

Six months later, Shanahan broke out the polygraph again in an attempt to clear troubled running back Travis Henry of a positive marijuana test. Henry had been the Broncos' big-ticket free-agent acquisition in 2007 and was among the league leaders in rushing before falling afoul of the league. The lie detector and a hairfollicle sample worked, and Henry was reinstated. But Shanahan's faith in Henry was not rewarded; the running back tested positive for marijuana the following off-season and was eventually convicted of involvement in a cocaine trafficking operation.

Henry was just one of numerous poor investments of guaranteed money in the latter years of the Shanahan era as he desperately attempted to build another championship team. Defensive end Simeon Rice, a Pro Bowler in Tampa Bay, lasted barely half of the 2007 season before being cut, but cost the Broncos $3 million and didn't even record a sack. Four years earlier, the Broncos had signed Daryl Gardener to a $34.8 million deal; he promptly broke his hand after getting into a fight at a nearby International House of Pancakes, started all of two games, and vented to a Denver radio talk show about being blackballed by "the little man upstairs."

There was little question of whom Gardener was speaking; he wasn't referring to the team's long-time janitor, a cheerful immigrant from Southeast Asia who whistled to himself, reminded late-lingering employees to lock the doors when they left, and treasured a picture on his desk of himself with Texas governor George W. Bush during a campaign stop at Dove Valley in the run-up to the 2000 presidential election.

Gardener was cut the following off-season, and the Broncos rarely wasted time letting a problem linger. But the consequences of such missteps was a looming salary-cap crunch that forced the Broncos to swallow their medicine in the 2008 off-season, with an underwhelming group of veteran newcomers that included seven unrestricted free agents, all but one of whom was expunged from the roster by 2009.

The fall of the House of Shanahan didn't happen all at once. But as with a rotting building, the damage accumulated. By the end of the 2008 season, the off-field issues, declining defense, free-agent and draft misfires, and late-season collapses were too much to bear. A three-game losing streak in which the Broncos blew three chances to clinch the AFC West ended with a 52-21 loss at San Diego that proved to be the final straw. Shanahan the coach was still capable of crating a superb game plan, but Shanahan the executive vice president was incapable of collecting enough players to properly execute it.

Eventually, the Broncos would return to the heights they reached early in Shanahan's tenure. But their decline was not done, and their fortunes grew far worse before they improved.

THE YOUNGEST COACH

That's not to say that the Josh McDaniels era did not begin with a sense of optimism. Hired at just thirty-two years of age, McDaniels was in the vanguard of young assistants without head coaching experience that were in vogue as the NFL's coaching carousel took its annual spin in 2009. McDaniels wasn't even the youngest coach hired in that round of hirings; Tampa Bay tapped position coach Raheem Morris to replace the fired Jon Gruden. Like Shanahan, Gruden was once a mastermind wunderkind, again proving the cyclical nature of the league's overall process.

But unlike Gruden and Shanahan, McDaniels struggled in adjusting to the big chair. One of his first moves was to sign long snapper Lonie Paxton from New England. Although Paxton was one of the league's best long snappers, the same could be said of Mike Leach, a popular player who joined the team midway through the 2002 season and had performed his job flawlessly for the next six-and-a-half seasons.

None of that mattered, as McDaniels wanted to remake the team his way. And when Leach was cast aside, it was clear there was a new boss in town and change was coming—even in spots where it was unnecessary.

Paxton was the first of a Broncos-record fourteen unrestricted free agents to be signed in McDaniels' first off-season. The best of these was Brian Dawkins, who the Philadelphia Eagles elected not to re-sign, largely because of his advancing age. The 2009 season would be his fourteenth in the league.

As with John Lynch a few years earlier, his straight-line speed wasn't what it was in his younger days. But just like Lynch, Dawkins compensated with a preternatural ability to read plays as they happened and an aggressive style that had always defined him. He finished his first Broncos season in the Pro Bowl.

Dawkins would be the bright spot of McDaniels' free-agent classes; he brought discipline, accountability and leadership to a locker room that needed all of it. In the previous three years, a generation of leaders had retired or moved on: Rod Smith, Jake Plummer, John Lynch, Al Wilson, Tom Nalen, Jason Elam.

"Dawk" will always be one of my favorite Broncos. He doesn't suffer fools, answers questions directly, and speaks with purpose. He has a bit of an edge to him, which underscores his sincerity; you can trust someone who looks you in the eye the way he does. Dawkins settled in the Denver area after his retirement and is a community treasure, working as a volunteer high school football coach and occasionally returning to Dove Valley to check up on his old team.

Dawkins would team with Champ Bailey to form the backbone of the secondary; their production and the pass-rush presence of Elvis Dumervil allowed new defensive coordinator Mike Nolan to quickly reverse the fortunes of a defense that had been in free fall in Shanahan's last two seasons.

But no personnel move under McDaniels would rattle the organization like the trade of quarterback Jay Cutler, who had grown into a Pro Bowler in his two-plus years as the starting quarterback. The 2008 Broncos had ninety-nine problems, and Cutler wasn't one. But a litany of hurt feelings and pointed fingers led to the trade on April 2, 2009, that sent Cutler and a fifth-round pick to Chicago in exchange for quarterback Kyle Orton, two first-round picks, and a third-rounder.

Without Cutler's howitzer right arm, the offense declined, falling from second in the league in 2008 to fifteenth. Wide receiver Brandon Marshall was capable of almost anything, from a league-record 21 receptions against the Colts in Week 14 to getting in trouble by punting a ball instead of handing it back to an equipment staffer in the preseason. Eventually, Marshall would be suspended for the final game of the regular season and would be traded the following off-season.

"STOKLEY! WOW!"

There wasn't an announcer in the English-speaking world more qualified to call the wackiest game-winning touchdown in Broncos history than Gus Johnson, then of CBS Sports. Known more for his borderline-not-quite-human screams of excitement at last-second baskets during the NCAA Tournament, Johnson has also called football games and was at the microphone for the first game of the McDaniels era, a trip to Cincinnati.

The game was desultory. The first returns on the new offense and Orton's stewardship of it were poor; as the final minute of regulation began, the Broncos had just six points and were staring at a one-point loss to a team that had gone 4-11-1 the year before.

With twenty-eight seconds remaining, the Broncos were at their 13-yard line, and had one timeout remaining. Even for cannon-legged Matt

Prater, the Broncos needed to gain 40 yards to give him a plausible long-range shot. Needing a clump of yardage, Orton threw into triple coverage for Marshall at the Denver 37-yard line, near the left sideline. Leon Hall leapt in front of Marshall and tipped the football above everyone—and into the grasp of wide receiver Brandon Stokley, who alertly trailed the play.

Stokley grabbed the football at the 44-yard line. He was past all three defenders, who had been occupied with Marshall. No one touched him. The only man in the stadium with a crazier reaction than the Broncos on the sideline was Johnson in the booth:

"Oh, Caught! Stokley! Down the Sideline! Can They Catch Him?! Stokley! Wow! Touchdown, Denver! Unbelievable! Oh My Goodness, What a Play!"

"It was pretty much a blur. Kind of a 'please don't get caught' type of thinking," Stokley recalled.

As Johnson convulsed, Stokley was the coolest man in the stadium. His football awareness is so keen that he got inside the Cincinnati 5-yard line and ran parallel to the goal line, consuming an extra five seconds from the clock before he stepped into the end zone.

"I just kind of saw that nobody was behind me chasing me," Stokley remembered. "I saw a guy kind of give up on it. I knew there wasn't a lot of time left, so I thought, 'Why not try to run some time off?'"

The Broncos won, 12-7, and the stunning result energized the Broncos. The defense continued to flourish, holding its first five opponents to just 43 points. The offense steadied, although it lacked the firepower of 2008. Marshall found his form. Elvis Dumervil, the team's best pass rusher, set a team record (since broken) with 17 sacks, as the Broncos converted him from 4-3 defensive end to 3-4 outside linebacker, which fit his 250-pound frame well.

But the buzz and good feelings faded. The Broncos became the first team to start 6-0 and not finish with a winning season since the 1978 Washington Redskins.

CHAPTER SIX

The 2010s

As the Broncos' sixth decade of play began, they were in the spot that NFL teams dread: mediocrity. The collapse of 2009 extended their run of years without a playoff appearance to four; in those seasons, the Broncos went 32-32. Mike Nolan, the coordinator who had helped resuscitate the defense in Josh McDaniels' first season, left to take the same job in Miami. The Broncos lost eight of their last ten games in 2009, frittering away what seemed to be a certain playoff spot, but what no one could see is that their fortunes were about to get even worse.

THE OVERLOOKED ORTON

Not since 1976, when Steve Ramsey started twelve games and Craig Penrose two, had a Broncos first-team quarterback been as unloved by the fans as Kyle Orton. Although Orton had a stellar statistical season in 2009, his average arm strength, reserved nature with the media and public, and predilection for late-game foibles did little to endear him to the fans.

Then the Broncos drafted Heisman Trophy-winner Tim Tebow, and all of a sudden Orton was yesterday's news, even though he was still the unquestioned starting quarterback. And while he appeared to be a bridge to the Tebow era, it appeared to be one as long as the spans that cross San Francisco Bay.

Tebow wasn't ready to start, and looked as through he wouldn't be for a long time. His elongated, awkward delivery didn't need refinement; it required a full-scale, ground-up reconstruction. Quarterbacks coach Ben McDaniels was given this task, and Tebow's inconsistent play in training camp revealed that it was going to take a while.

But on the hillside above the practice field, Tebow's moment had already arrived. His jersey was among the league's biggest sellers, drawing the wallets of long-time Broncos fans hopeful for his progress and a sizable chunk of evangelical Christians from around the nation who admired the religious values that Tebow displayed; many had latched onto him at the University of Florida and were going to follow him, wherever he landed. For as long as Tebow remained in a Broncos uniform, these two groups coexisted. It wasn't always easy; some long-time Broncos supporters resented the newcomers, knowing that many would move on if and when Tebow was no longer on the team.

To the Tebow fans, Orton was the guy blocking their man's ascension to the starting job. To the Broncos fans, Orton was in purgatory: he wasn't bad enough to merit sympathy, but not skilled enough to embrace. When Orton looked up to the fans, he saw Cutler jerseys, Elway jerseys, and Tebow jerseys.

One day that summer, I accompanied fellow long-time Broncos scribe Lee Rasizer on a search for Orton jerseys at the merchandise trailer set up outside the fans' entrance to training camp. None were for sale.

Of course, there were some made, and to this day, you see the occasional Orton jersey fished out of the closet and worn. But despite throwing 49 touchdown passes against 28 interceptions and averaging 250.4 yards per start, he never captured Denver, and he is remembered only for a 12-21 record as a starter that is the worst for a Broncos quarterback to start at least two seasons since the AFL days.

Overwhelmed, Overpowered, Overmatched

In their first fifty-four seasons, the Broncos had fourteen head coaches. And all of those that took the job after the 1960s rise of the despised Raiders learned that if you're going to keep your job, you can't get demolished by the Raiders in front of the home fans.

A 48-16 loss to the then-Los Angeles Raiders in Week 4 of the 1994 season was the death knell for Wade Phillips. He was in just his second year on the job and had guided the Broncos to a wild-card play-off berth the previous season, but the defeat was the fourth consecutive loss to the Raiders on his watch, and dropped Denver to 0-4.

But that game was taut and competitive compared to what befell the befuddled McDaniels and his Broncos on October 24, 2010. A week earlier, Denver had lost a 24-20 heartbreaker to the New York Jets after a controversial pass-interference penalty against Renaldo Hill set up LaDainian Tomlinson's game-winning touchdown run. Buoyed by a strong performance against a team headed to its second consecutive AFC Championship Game, the 2-4 Broncos prepared to face the Raiders knowing that similar performances could get them back to .500 by their Week 9 bye.

Then came perhaps the worst minute of play the Broncos have ever endured, beginning with eleven minutes left in the first quarter.

It started when Oakland tight end Zach Miller ran counter to the flow on a Jason Campbell playfake, moved into the secondary past Joe Mays and D.J. Williams, and had nothing but open field because free safety Renaldo Hill had followed other Oakland targets who moved right, leaving the left deep area completely open. Nobody was within 10 yards of Miller, and he caught an easy touchdown.

On the ensuing possession, Kyle Orton's first pass of the game was intercepted by Oakland cornerback Chris Johnson, who jumped on Jabar Gaffney's out route, read Orton's eyes, and returned it 30 yards for a touchdown. The Broncos' next offensive play was a disastrous end-around that Demaryius Thomas fumbled and Lamarr Houston recovered.

By then, the clock read 10:02. Darren McFadden's first of four touchdowns—which came three plays and 64 seconds after Thomas's fumble—made the game a 21-0 rout that only worsened from there.

A sold-out crowd was shocked into silence by that disastrous 58 seconds. But as the Raiders built their advantage steadily through the 30s and 40s, shock was replaced by anger, and boos flooded the premises.

Worse yet, the Raiders took pity on the Broncos. They pulled most of their starters, including Campbell and McFadden, with an entire quarter left to play. Had the Raiders kept their engine in fifth gear, they had a chance to deal the Broncos the worst loss by any NFL team in seventy years, since the Chicago Bears' 73-0 shellacking of the Washington Redskins in the 1940 NFL Championship Game. Instead, the Raiders went scoreless in the fourth quarter and settled for a 59-14 pounding that wasn't as close as the score indicated.

"I take full responsibility for it. It's not good enough—it's not even close to good enough. I apologize to Pat (Bowlen) and the organization, all the fans and everyone else," a shocked McDaniels said, just moments after being booed off the field by the hardy remnants of a sellout crowd, nearly all of which had left by the start of the fourth quarter. "It was awful."

Dating back to the previous season, it was the Broncos' thirteenth loss in seventeen games. The team was in its worst slump since the last days of Lou Saban. It seemed the Broncos' predicament couldn't get any worse. A week later, it did.

Low Tide in London

When the NFL announced that the Broncos and 49ers would play the fourth regular-season game to take place at Wembley Stadium in as many years, the excitement was palpable. It had been eleven years since the Broncos played a preseason game overseas; from 1987-1999, they had played seven preseason games outside the United States, traveling to London, Berlin, Barcelona, Mexico City, Sydney and, on two occasions, Tokyo. Better yet, the Broncos would get a neutral-site game out of a game originally scheduled for creaky, drafty Candlestick Park.

What no one realized was that this weekend would see the franchise reach an even lower point than it did the previous weekend against the Raiders—and its lowest ebb altogether.

It wasn't just that the Broncos lost to a 1-6 San Francisco 49ers team starting a backup quarterback, or that the two teams spent a desultory first half exchanging miscues and convincing no British sports fan to give up soccer, cricket, or rugby for the United States' brand of football. Nor was it the mounting mistakes in the fourth quarter that handed the game to the 49ers, who would eventually finish in last place in arguably the worst single-season division in modern NFL history, a quartet so bad that 7-9 was good enough to win it.

It was what happened the day before the game. The two teams held walk-through practices at Wembley; first the Broncos, then the 49ers. That led to a video camera left running by team video director Steve Scarnecchia, recording the 49ers' session. It wasn't as though the illicit intelligence helped; the Broncos lost, 24-16. But when news of the incident broke three weeks later, the Broncos' already reeling reputation absorbed a devastating hit: the stain of cheating.

"This cuts into the trust of so many different constituents," said Joe Ellis, the team's chief operating officer at the time.

A 4-12 finish, the worst record since the AFL-NFL merger was bad. But seasons like that happen to every franchise in a league whose competitive model is built on creating parity. Since the expansion to a 16-game schedule in 1978, only the Pittsburgh Steelers have not had a season that finished 4-12 or worse. The 2010 season is the only one like it that the Broncos have endured; most clubs have a handful of such seasons, or more.

You can live with the on-field losses, even one as bad as the 45-point mauling the Raiders handed the Broncos four days before their 747 left for London. But the loss of honor? That was the biggest defeat the franchise could fathom.

Media quickly dubbed the incident "Spygate II," as a follow-up to the Patriots' illicit videotaping of Jets coaches in 2007. After news broke, it was no longer a matter of if McDaniels would be dismissed, but when. Attendance was starting to fall; one day after the tape scandal became public, there were more than 15,000 no-shows for a home loss to the St. Louis Rams. The only relevant question left was whether McDaniels coach out the season or be sent packing before Christmas.

The answer came late in the afternoon of December 6, one day after a closer-than-expected 10-6 loss to eventual AFC West champion Kansas City. McDaniels had already conducted his day-after-game press conference and was reviewing the previous day's game when he was sent home. With a wave to a photographer from behind the wheel of his SUV, McDaniels was gone.

"There wasn't any point delaying it," said Ellis.

THE RETURN OF ELWAY

Eric Studesville was the Broncos' head coach for just four games, going 1-3 as the interim boss after McDaniels' dismissal. In that short time, he cleansed the organization of the bitter aftertaste left from the last months of the McDaniels era. That helped establish the first-year Broncos coach in the organization, and he endured through the subsequent changes and remains the team's running backs coach.

But for fundamental change, and to restore the luster of the Broncos in the community, there was only one name that mattered. And when reports leaked late in the 2010 season that the Broncos were talking to John Elway about returning to run the club's football operations, Denver held its breath with anticipation.

What would Elway be like as an executive?

Believe it or not, the answers were evident even before he stepped to the lectern and addressed the media for the first time as executive vice president of football operations.

It helped that he had run the Arena Football League's Colorado Crush for its six-season run, from 2003 to 2008. The Crush won a league championship and ranked among the Arena League's attendance leaders. But the team's first year was a 2-14 disaster. That forced Elway to make the kind of tough decision that NFL executives must make: he fired coach Bob Beers, a long-time family friend who had worked as a Broncos scout before giving the Crush a whirl.

The collapse and restructuring of the league brought down the curtain on the Crush. But by that time, Elway was ready for the big field and the big chair. He learned on the job, but leaned on the lessons from club holdovers like Matt Russell and his late father Jack, a former coach and Broncos personnel director.

The other key item in Elway's background was his work in automotive sales. He watched over a small empire of dealerships with the John Elway name. In that capacity he proved that he could close a sale—a talent that would be a crucial asset in attracting elite free agents.

His first task was simple: he needed a coach.

Calling on Fox to Pick up the Pieces

The No. 2 pick the Broncos held in the 2011 draft was the highest in club history since the first common AFL-NFL draft of 1967, and was evidence to the depths to which the Broncos had fallen. The only team picking ahead of the Broncos were the Carolina Panthers, whose season was irrelevant to the Broncos—until their own season ended.

It was by far the worst season that head coach John Fox had endured. In his first eight seasons stalking the south sideline in Charlotte, he earned a reputation for motivation and supervising game plans that minimized the exposure of his team's weaknesses. Sometimes they were overmatched, but they usually kept the game close. In one memorable 2002 game, Fox was forced to start Randy Fasani at quarterback against the Tampa Bay Buccaneers, who were halfway to their only world championship. Fasani was so bad that his quarterback rating was 0.0, a number last heard when Dean Wormer was reading grade-point averages to Delta Tau Chi in *Animal House*. Yet in spite of that, the Panthers gave the Bucs one of their toughest games and only fell on a last-minute field goal. A year later, Fox had tweaked the roster, and the Panthers went to the Super Bowl, and remained competitive for seven more seasons until going 2-14 in 2010.

That finish came under extenuating circumstances. In advance of the end of the collective bargaining agreement and expected lockout in the 2011 off-season, Panthers management had spent the first months of 2010 trimming salaries, gutting the veteran leadership of a team that as recently as January 2009 had the NFC's best record, and was hosting a divisional playoff game. Players like Jake Delhomme, Julius Peppers, and Brad Hoover were a part of Fox's teams going back to his first Super Bowl run in 2003, and were purged or allowed to sign elsewhere. Injuries to expected starting quarterback Matt Moore hastened the spiral. By November 2010, Fox was forced to resort to signing journeyman quarterback Brian St. Pierre off the street and starting him four days later against the playoff-bound Ravens. Somehow, Fox managed to keep the Panthers' locker room from crumbling; the team played hard until the end, even though he was a lame duck, coaching in the final year of his contract.

During the 2008 and 2009 seasons, I wrote for the Panthers' website, Panthers.com. One day in the 2008 off-season, while watching practice with other reporters, a few of us got into an animated conversation about Fox. Since I was new, the locals wanted my outsiders' perspective on Fox. My reply was quick: "Who are you going to find that's better? If the Panthers let him go, he'll have another head-coaching job within a week."

I was wrong. It wasn't a week. But ten days after Fox left Bank of America Stadium for the final time as Panthers head coach, he stood in the team meeting room at Dove Valley, beaming in an orange tie as Elway introduced him as the newest coach of the Broncos.

It was a job he had done before. In 2002, he took over a Panthers team that had gone 1-15. Nine years later, would be tasked with putting together a locker room that was equally shattered by defeat and dissension.

But in both cases, Fox did not believe a total teardown was in order. This was in stark contrast to McDaniels, who in 2009 took an offense that had been among the league's leaders and jettisoned its quarterback. Instead, Fox and his staff watched tape and evaluated. As was the case with Carolina, he knew that his rebuilding plan would be one step ahead if he could identify and retain the pieces that were functional. This wasn't a clear-cutting; this was a surgical rebuilding plan. And it didn't take long for it to get results—although they didn't happen in the way the Broncos intended.

2011: TEBOW TIME

A new coach and Elway upstairs did not make Broncos fans patient. By the fifth game of the season, they were howling.

Kyle Orton, still starting at quarterback, was in a funk. Two weeks earlier, he had thrown an interception to end a potential game-tying drive in a 17-14 loss at Tennessee. Seven days after that, he tossed three interceptions, one of which was returned for a touchdown, in a 49-23 beatdown at Green Bay. Finally, in the first half against San Diego, he threw another interception, had completed just six of 13 passes for 34 yards, and was only within 23-10 because Denver's defense had a pick-six of its own.

Meanwhile, Tim Tebow held the clipboard. He had started the last three games of 2010, but was relegated to the bench after Fox took over. Tebow's passing mechanics remained awkward and unorthodox, and the off-season lockout had wiped out the practices Tebow needed to refine his play. But the crowd wanted the blood of its starting quarterback. Orton was 12-20 as the Broncos' starter, and the fans had seen enough.

It was Tebow Time. After a balky third quarter, he started to improvise in the fourth, with the Broncos trailing 26-10 and nothing to lose. His scrambling kept plays alive and wore down pass rushers—and also the offensive line, which had to maintain its blocks for ever-lengthening periods. The Broncos lost, but after trailing by 16 with seven minutes remaining, a 29-24 defeat that came down to the last play felt like a win.

Orton was done and would be released the next month. The rest of 2011 was to be defined by Tebow, and how it impacted the offense, the team, and culture at large.

Within the locker room, the main issue revolved around masking the holes in his game. He couldn't run a traditional offense that was predicated on short timing routes. Offensive coordinator Mike McCoy went to work designing a run-first scheme that emphasized the zone-read option. Passing became a change-of-pace tactic, focused on deep routes designed to try and keep the safeties and cornerbacks honest and prevent them from crowding into the box.

To say the offense was a work in progress was an understatement. Few coaches and teams in modern NFL history have ever junked an entire scheme on the fly. But it was necessary to try and save the season. For the Broncos to work, the risk of big mistakes had to be minimized, and the defense had to complement it by preventing big plays and when in duress, holding opponents to field goals.

By November, the Broncos started to win. Tebow still struggled with accuracy, and his completion percentage of 46.3 was the worst for a quarterback with at least 250 passes since Cincinnati's Akili Smith in 2000. Considering that a typical baseline in the modern NFL is 60 percent, the Broncos couldn't throw often and sustain any hopes of victory.

But the defense tightened. During a six-game winning streak, four opponents scored 13 points or less; in those games, the defense allowed 10 touchdowns and 10 field goals. In an increasingly pass-happy league, the Broncos ran 68.7 percent of the time, and in a win at Kansas City passed just eight times and kept the football on the ground 55.

It worked to sneak the Broncos into the playoffs with a modest 8-8 finish, which Tebow followed with his best game, a 10-for-15, 316-yard performance in a wild-card win over the Steelers. But that game was the exception toward the end of the 2011 season, and his late-year struggles offered a sign that the league had caught up to the Broncos' gambit.

THE MASTER FINDS NEW APPRENTICES

After John Elway returned to the Broncos as executive vice president in 2011, he and head coach John Fox opened the doors to former Broncos to come watch practice, talk to players, and be mentors. Some, like Karl Mecklenburg, have even worked with position groups in practice. Others have spoken to the team after practice with messages of wisdom and motivation.

But perhaps no Bronco delights more in this role than Rod Smith. Three years after he retired in 2008 following hip-replacement surgery, he was an occasional presence with the wide receivers. Following the midseason trade of disgruntled Pro Bowler Brandon Lloyd to the St. Louis Rams, the group left behind was young. Fourth-year veteran Eddie Royal was the closest thing to a grizzled presence. The group's long-term hopes were in the hands of 2010 draft picks Demaryius Thomas and Eric Decker.

And when Smith walked into Broncos headquarters to meet his successors the week after Thanksgiving in 2011, he found a dispirited bunch. With the offense overhauled to fit Tebow's skill set, the precision timing of the passing game of the previous two-and-a-half seasons had been junked. Passes became scarcer than evergreens above a Rocky Mountain tree line.

"I said, 'Guys, that part, you don't control,'" Smith recalled. "'You control how you come out of the huddle, how you run your route. You control that. You control blocking in the run game.

"'I know it sucks. It sucks to be a receiver and not know if you're going to get the ball, ever. You never know. But what makes you a champion is when you go out there thinking it's coming to you anyway and you go out there and go to work.'"

No one took those words to heart like Thomas, whose glimpses of brilliance had been rare to that point. Some pundits were even calling the 2010 first-rounder a bust, after just sixteen career games played. He'd caught just three passes for 66 yards in the previous four games and had missed the first month of the season because of a fractured pinkie, which followed a torn Achilles tendon suffered in an off-season workout. He missed time as a rookie following an ankle injury suffered in a preseason scrimmage. Thomas had not dazzled, but he had never really had the chance, either.

The following weekend, the Broncos traveled to Minnesota to play in the Metrodome for the final time. Against the Vikings, Thomas broke out with his biggest game to date—four catches, 144 yards, and two touchdowns—helping break the offense out of a funk and carrying the Broncos to a 35-32 win.

Even though the passing game was limited with Tebow at the controls, Thomas flourished. In the last seven games of the 2011 season, he grabbed thirty-five passes for 645 yards and four touchdowns. When Peyton Manning signed with the Broncos in the following off-season, Thomas' progress continued. He was selected for the next two Pro Bowls and emerged as one of the game's elite receivers. In doing so, he became the heir to Smith's franchise-record-breaking legacy.

"Whether it helped out, I don't know, but his approach seemed different from that day forward," Smith said.

"I Don't Have a 'Plan B'"

It wouldn't be long before Smith wouldn't need to give those kinds of pick-me-up speeches to wide receivers. Not with Peyton Manning around.

In February 2012, the notion of Manning in orange and blue seemed unfathomable. The Colts seemed likely to cut him to make way for Andrew Luck, and they did. But Tebow had galvanized many fans, and his energetic play and frequent, visible displays of his evangelical Christian faith had tapped into a significant market. There were Broncos fans, and there were Tebow fans, and the Venn diagram between the two groups didn't overlap as many would have hoped.

The Broncos had indicated they were in the market for a quarterback, to at least provide competition for Tebow, if not supplant him. In early March, Broncos brass hopped on a private plane to fly to Stillwater, Oklahoma, to watch Oklahoma State quarterback Brandon Weeden work out. But after the plane dropped off the Denver contingent, it flew to Miami to pick up Manning. On its return to Denver, it stopped for Elway, Fox, and their associates.

Thus began the pursuit of Peyton Manning. They met with him, talked football strategy with the offensive coaches, went out to dinner. And then they let him be until he called their phone again, scheduling a time to come watch a workout.

The Colts had cut Manning and Elway and Fox could tell he was still stunned. The hard sell would not work. They had to let Manning come to his choice in his own time. Don't come on strong.

"It was a pretty emotional day for him—as it would be for just about anybody, let alone a guy that had been somewhere for fourteen years," Fox said. "I was respectful of that.

"I was really just seeing how he was doing and what his plans were. I didn't know what plans he had or any of those types of things. It was a conversation."

After that, again, Elway and Fox let Manning marinate on the choices in front of him: Denver, Tennessee, or San Francisco.

Three days after the workout and ten days after Manning's visit, Fox was in Elway's office, talking personnel matters. The phone rang.

"I think we both froze," Elway said.

He picked it up. Manning's voice came through the line.

"He says, 'It has kind of been a rough morning because I've had to call these other teams and say I'm not going to go work for them,'" Elway recalled.

"And he said, 'I want to play for the Denver Broncos.'"

The Broncos had put their short-term future in Manning's hands. The only criticism of the deal rested upon the state of Manning's neck and nerves following multiple neck surgeries in the previous year.

When Manning was introduced, Elway was asked about a contingency plan if Manning's health faltered—a "Plan B."

"Plan B? I don't have a Plan B," laughed Elway. "We're going with Plan A."

That plan immediately vaulted the Broncos back to prominence.

TALKING ABOUT PRACTICE

One aspect of Denver's adoration for its Broncos was something Manning wasn't expecting—and didn't seem to appreciate much: the intense, hyper-focus local media places on even the most mundane of work: the off-season organized team activities held each May and June.

"I've never had to comment before on incompletions in practice before, so this is new to me," he said bemusedly during his second post-practice press conference during the 2012 off-season.

The number of newspapers covering the Broncos shrunk over the years. As recently as 2005, five newspapers—*The Denver Post*, *Rocky Mountain News*, *The* (Boulder) *Daily Camera*, *Longmont Times-Call*, and *The Gazette* from Colorado Springs covered each practice and game, no matter where it was played. This gave the Broncos one of the league's bigger beat-writing contingents. By the time Manning arrived, the *Rocky* had succumbed to mounting industry pressures and folded, and the newspapers from Colorado Springs, Longmont, and Boulder had pruned their budgets and cut back to covering the college teams in their backyards.

But radio and the Internet filled the void. By the time Manning arrived, Denver had four sports-radio stations which talked Broncos daily for twelve months a year. There could be nothing transpiring in the NFL, and it could be the heart of the seasons for the NBA's Nuggets, MLB's Rockies, and NHL's Avalanche; too often, it didn't matter.

This was a bit different from Indianapolis, where the Colts' following is devoted but Indiana's pulse quickens to the beat of the bouncing basketball at high schools and colleges throughout Hoosierland. Manning made the state stand at attention for the Colts and cemented their place on that state's sports landscape, but Colts football trails both basketball and open-wheel auto racing when most think of the sport for which Indiana is best known.

John Fox learned this when he arrived in Denver from a nine-year stint in Carolina a year earlier. Broncos football matters twelve months a year. There is no off-season for scrutiny.

GIDDY FOR PEYTON

The adulation for Tim Tebow at the two previous training camps surpassed anything since John Elway's retirement following the 1998 season. But that paled again when compared with the reception Peyton Manning received upon taking the field each day for the 2012 training camp.

Every completion—heck, every step onto the practice field—was greeted with applause. It didn't matter if Manning was not throwing against a defense or if he was in the quarter-speed walk-through periods that start each camp session. And practice ended and Manning sauntered over to the grassy knoll where upwards of 2,000 fans watched each day's practice, it was as though Manning was John Lennon, Paul McCartney, George Harrison, and Ringo Starr all rolled into one, and he was at JFK Airport, reaching out to the hordes of giddy onlookers.

But sometimes, the fan adulation was misinterpreted. When then-rookie defensive lineman Derek Wolfe hit the field for his first training-camp practice that summer, he thought the cheers were for him. After all, he was the top pick in that year's draft class and a projected starter—the fans could be calling for him, right?

"When we came out here, I was right in front of Manning and I didn't know it," Wolfe said. "They made a pretty big fuss, and I was like, 'Why are they yelling so crazy for me?' Then I looked behind me and it was Manning standing there."

And just by standing there, Manning drew an ovation. Never has someone received so much appreciation simply for showing up. But that was only the beginning for Manning; he was about to start rewriting the single-season passing section of the Broncos' record book.

JOHN FOX'S HAPPY RETURN

Although Fox relocated to Colorado, he kept his home in Charlotte. His ties still ran deep in North Carolina. So even though he publicly proclaimed that the Broncos' trip to Carolina for a game on November 12, 2012, was no big deal, it was something different.

The Panthers had struggled since his departure and that continued in a 36-14 Denver romp. Fox was on the opposite sideline, but looked as comfortable as ever; in fact, the weirdest part of the day came when he walked onto the field and nearly took the tunnel that the home team uses.

"It was odd leaving out of that tunnel," he said. "I've been through the other one a bunch of times. In fact, I kind of steered to the right by accident until I finally figured out I have to go the other way."

After the game, Fox left the field to cheers from fans who appreciated his nine years in Carolina. Pat Bowlen gave Fox the game ball. He stopped in the hallways throughout the service level of the stadium to greet Panthers employees and friends he'd made.

But he would be back in Charlotte again. On November 2, 2013, Fox was enjoying a bye-weekend round of golf when he felt dizzy and had to lie down. Fox was scheduled for aortic-valve replacement surgery after the season, but after he was stricken on the 14th hole at Quail Hollow Club, the procedure couldn't wait.

"God, you get me out of this, and I'll get it fixed now," he said.

Fortunately, he was in the right place.

"Luckily, I was 200 yards from my backyard playing with two friends that are our neighbors," Fox said. "You know, I could have been sixty miles out fishing on my boat in Marco (Island, Florida), and that would not have been too good. So this was great, it was just the timing of it. The good Lord was looking out for me for sure."

He missed four games; the Broncos won three with interim head coach Jack Del Rio at the helm. But he stayed involved. He watched practice footage on the iPad playbooks given to all players and coaches. He talked to coaches over the phone. But on game days, he sat down, took notes, and dealt with the emotion of being powerless to affect the outcome.

TRINDON HOLLIDAY: A BIT OF A FLIPPANT RETURNER

Rick Upchurch is the best returner in Broncos history, but even he was not as electric as 5-foot-5 Trindon Holliday in November 2012. Holliday was a waiver claim from the Houston Texans a month earlier and had enough straight-line speed to have qualified for the U.S. Olympic trials in 2008. But Holliday darted between delight and disaster and fumbled, on average, once every nine returns as a Bronco.

The jagged edge on which Holliday ran was most evident in that win over Carolina. Holliday scored for the second consecutive week, having returned the opening kickoff of the second half for a touchdown at Cincinnati to start the road swing. But on this punt return, he casually flipped the football across the goal line as he crossed it.

This celebration was a habit—a bad one—and the Broncos were fortunate it did not cost them at least one touchdown. When he flipped the football at Carolina, it bounced out of the end zone and replays showed it should have been a touchback, since he appeared to have not broken the plane of the end zone.

"I thought I had crossed the goal line," Holliday said. "(Special teams) coach (Jeff Rodgers) told me, 'Next time I cross the goal line, just bring him the football.'"

ONE MOMENT TO FORGET

In the final minute of the fourth quarter of their 2012 divisional play-off game, all the Broncos had to do was stop the Baltimore Ravens one more time. Leading 35-28, and with a frenzied, if frozen, home crowd behind them, the Ravens had to go 70 yards, with the clock ticking below forty seconds.

But the one thing that Baltimore quarterback Joe Flacco does well, above all, is throw it deep. He uncorked a pass deep and high into the 8-degree night. Instead of keeping intended target Jacoby Jones in front of him, Rahim Moore let Jones get behind him, playing the ball. When the ball instead sailed beyond his grasp, he—and the Broncos—were sunk. Catch, touchdown, 70 yards. Thirty-one seconds remained in regulation, and much of Colorado was in a state of shock.

"I just misjudged it. I let it get over my head, first of all, when I could have just do what I do best, and that's watch the flight of the ball, and I didn't do that right," said Moore.

Cornerback Champ Bailey thought Moore misjudged it because Flacco sent it on a high arc.

"Yeah, it was, and that's the way Flacco throws. He'll throw some up like that," Bailey said. "They are hard to judge, but I know that's a play Rahim will make ninety-nine times out of a hundred."

Unfortunately, that was the one exception. But the Broncos would not have been in that position without other mistakes—a lost fumble, an interception returned for a touchdown by Corey Graham, two deep touchdown passes from Flacco to Torrey Smith in the first half, and a field-goal attempt by Matt Prater in which his foot caught a divot of the frozen turf. Take away any one of those, and the Broncos would have gone to the AFC Championship Game for the ninth time.

Instead, the Broncos eventually fell in double overtime, 38-35, in what was the most crushing defeat absorbed by the club since the loss to Jacksonville in the same playoff round sixteen years earlier. It was the longest game the club had ever played, but it would feel far lengthier in the months that followed, as the Broncos tried to use it as motivation for the next season rather than lament an opportunity lost.

After the game, Moore briefly met the media, choking back tears as he did so. It would have been easy for the young safety to duck into the trainer's room and avoid the cameras and recorders, but he didn't. He apologized to Broncos fans, his voice quaking with emotion.

"I'll tell the fans that we fought our hearts out, and it was my fault," he said, choking back tears. "It was my fault. If they wouldn't have scored on us on that last play, we'd be in here rejoicing. If people don't like me after that, I'm sorry, but I feel like that was my fault and I'm going to take full responsibility of it."

And then he spent the off-season working to atone for that mistake.

Moore is a perfectionist, which fit well in the locker-room culture that Manning helped fortify in 2012. If you ask him a question in which you compliment his play, don't be surprised if he offers multiple reasons why it wasn't as good as you believed it was.

Unfortunately, he would not have the chance to make up for the playoff misplay. Ten games into the following season, he pulled up when trying to chase down Kansas City running back Jamaal Charles in a *Sunday Night Football* duel. Moore left the Broncos in 2015 for Houston, where he spent one season with the Texans.

FROM HOOPS TO HORSES

Julius Thomas' emergence as one of the game's best receiving tight ends in 2013 capped one of the most unusual trajectories any Bronco has taken to an NFL career. Thomas played just one year of college football at Portland State University before being drafted and prior to that had not played since his freshman year of high school. In between those years, he concentrated on basketball and was a starting power forward at PSU, which plays in the Big Sky Conference.

But at least he had one year in college football. That was more than could be said in 2005 for Wesley Duke, whom the Broncos signed as an undrafted free agent from Mercer University in Macon, Georgia. Duke couldn't play football in college because Mercer did not even have a football team.

Duke had not played football since high school, but after being signed to play tight end, he didn't back away from a challenge. Given a choice of three jersey numbers by the Broncos—39, 49, or 84—he chose 84, which Shannon Sharpe had worn for twelve seasons in breaking all franchise receiving records among tight ends.

"I wanted to catch touchdowns," Duke said. "I said, 'Give me 84.'"

In Week 15 at Buffalo, he did. His first NFL reception was a 1-yard touchdown catch from Jake Plummer in a 28-17 win that clinched the Broncos' third consecutive playoff spot. He celebrated the score by what looked like a failed dunk off the crossbar but what he later claimed was a "power layup."

"Next time, I might stick my elbow (up)," he said.

Unfortunately for Duke, there wouldn't be a next time. Although he started in the AFC Championship Game a month later, he suffered a fourth tear of his left anterior cruciate ligament in an off-season practice the following spring, and was released. The other three injuries had come in college.

Decades before Duke's year in orange and blue, the Broncos attempted to turn a pair of Atlantic Coast Conference basketball standouts into football players. In 1983, they selected former Clemson point guard Murray Jarman with a twelfth-round pick. Jarman's primary claim to fame was that he scored 28 points against a North Carolina team that featured future NBA stalwarts Sam Perkins, Brad Daugherty, and Michael Jordan. Jarman didn't make it through the preseason.

Seven years later, the team signed ex-Georgia Tech starting guard Karl Brown to play cornerback and former Ball State forward Paris McCurdy, who was installed as a linebacker. Neither lasted through the summer.

The Broncos watched Brown play for the Yellow Jackets in that year's Final Four, held in McNichols Sports Arena. He was 6-foot-2 and 185 pounds, lithe, and athletic. With a long wingspan, he possessed a physical tool that scouts today still look for in a cornerback. But his experience with the sport was even less than others who hadn't played it in college; he was raised in England, where football meant corner kicks, headers, and a round ball.

"I looked at football, I looked at school, I looked at basketball. Basketball won out," Brown said at the time. He eventually played a decade in Europe and since 2004 has run and coached a basketball team in his hometown, the Leicester Warriors.

But before them all, there was a basketball player who did make it as a Bronco: defensive back Lonnie Wright, who was with the Broncos from 1966 to 1967. A member of the 1964 U.S. Olympic basketball team that participated in the Tokyo Games, Wright played pro basketball and football in the same season when he joined the ABA's Denver Rockets—later to be rechristened the Nuggets. The Broncos left Wright unprotected in the 1968 expansion draft, and the Cincinnati Bengals claimed him, but he never played a down, opting to stay in Denver and continue with the Rockets for four more years.

"Only" Preseason? Not to Elway

The tempo and tenor of preseason football usually prevents beat-downs. Sometimes it's because one team gets an early lead and throttles back, not wanting to risk its key players to injury; at others, teams want to get a look at specific plays and personnel groupings in particular scenarios, so they might not run what would be their typical tactic when the games count.

But August 17, 2013, in Seattle was nothing like that—at least not to the young, energetic Seahawks. The visit from Peyton Manning and the Broncos was their chance to make a statement. From the sidelines to the last row, they and their fans did. In all three phases, Seattle's players appeared to have been propelled by slingshot. They hit Manning, with Bobby Wagner drilling the quarterback after a missed block. They forced a fumble at the goal line. The crowd was raucous—louder and more hostile than any other road venue for the Broncos that season. They scored on offense, defense, and special teams in a 40-10 rout that was not as close as the score indicated.

In the locker room after the game, the Broncos weren't furious. Some things went wrong, but it was just preseason. There was more worry over the state of Champ Bailey's left foot, which he injured late in the first half, than the way they played the game.

Then they walked into Dove Valley for a team meeting after a Sunday off. Waiting for them was Elway; this was the first hint that something was amiss. He had not addressed the entire team during the previous season.

Manning alertly whipped out his notepad. So did many teammates. What they got was a verbal evisceration and a reminder that there were great expectations that had to be met—even in the games that didn't count.

"John pretty much laid it on us," Manning said. "He was not happy with that game. It was a butt-kicking, and whether it's preseason or regular season, he was just sharing his thoughts that that won't be accepted under his role as kind of the leader of this organization along with Pat Bowlen."

After an off-season in which players and coaches had spoken at length about the extra motivation stemming from the previous January's divisional-playoff loss, "Especially coming off the Baltimore loss, I didn't care if it was preseason or regular season, you never go someplace and play like we played up in Seattle and really not care about that and say, 'It's OK,' because if you're competitive, and we want to be as good as we want to be, then that attitude does not transcend to any game," Elway said.

The meeting was not a turning point, but it was a reminder: everyone would gun for the Broncos. Great expectations were back in Denver, but great efforts would be required, too.

"He just said that it was just not acceptable with that type of game, talking to the entire team—the starters played the first quarter and a half, the second, third, and fourth guys—so he was talking to everyone," he continued. "It was a full-on alert that it's not an acceptable performance.

"I think it was a challenge, too, that he saw some real potential in this team, he thought it had the makings of a special team and just wanted to be sure we were going to max out."

Given that the Broncos would end the season with their first Super Bowl trip in fifteen years, the speech worked.

RECORD AFTER RECORD FALLS

Manning is as consistent in his statements as he is in his play. Throughout his first two off-seasons in Denver, he reminded anyone who listened that getting the proper timing with a new set of receivers takes years. Thus, it would inevitably be better in 2013 than 2012, as the practice repetitions with targets like Demaryius Thomas, Eric Decker, and Julius Thomas accumulated.

But how much better?

Try the best season of Manning's career. A seven-touchdown performance in the season opener gave Manning the first of a slew of NFL records he would own or extend by the end of 2013: touchdown passes in a single season (55), passing yards in a single season (5,477), career MVP awards (five), game-winning drives in the regular season or overtime (50), and seasons with at least twelve wins (10).

The Broncos scored more points than any offense in league history. Diverse in its array of playmakers, it became the only offense in which five players scored at least 10 touchdowns. Even in an era of turbo-charged numbers, the Broncos' production was absurdly prolific: 606 points in the regular season, an average of 37.9 per game.

Another major NFL record was set by a Bronco in 2013: the 64-yard field goal drilled by Matt Prater against the Tennessee Titans on December 8. Prater broke the record 63-yard kick set by New Orleans' Tom Dempsey in 1970 and later matched by three other players, including Jason Elam in 1998.

So much has to go right for the opportunity to hit a long field goal: the attempt has to come at the end of a half, reducing the consequences of a miss from long distance, and the kicker needs to be strong—or perhaps be booting at mile-high altitude. Of the five field goals covering at least 63 yards, three were in Denver. And in 2002, Ola Kimrin hit a 65-yard attempt for the Broncos in the preseason finale against Seattle.

FINALLY, CHAMP GETS THE GAME HE DESERVES

As Champ Bailey grappled with a foot injury most of the 2013 season, an air of finality engulfed the best cornerback in Broncos history. He had been left grasping on a pair of touchdowns in the previous year's playoff loss to Baltimore. The structure of his contract made a potential renegotiation or an outright release painless under the salary cap, and in his 15th NFL season, he was reaching territory that few cornerbacks had ever known.

When he finally returned in December after exacerbating the injury in two separate returns to action, he was limited to work in the Broncos' nickel and dime packages, placing a natural cap on his repetitions. That reality was as painful as the foot for a cornerback who prided himself on being left on an island to cover an opponent's top receiver without needing much help from a safety.

His role looked as though it would be limited until Chris Harris Jr. suffered a partial knee ligament tear in the divisional-round win over the Chargers. With no other proven options, Bailey was back to playing every down, and in the AFC Championship Game delivered a vintage, lockdown performance moving between the slot and outside.

"Man, he played an outstanding game against the Patriots," said Brian Dawkins, two years into retirement but still an occasional presence around Dove Valley.

As the Broncos celebrated the 26-16 win over the Patriots, there was an abundance of happiness. For John Fox, having overcome his health scare and surgery. For Manning, becoming just the third quarterback to take multiple teams to the Super Bowl. For players, who had overcome their own personal obstacles to make it to this point.

But above all, this Super Bowl trip was for Bailey, who had carried the defense through lean years, re-signed with the Broncos when they were at their 4-12 nadir, and now was a part of getting them back to the pinnacle.

"There are a lot of guys in that (locker) room (for whom) it means a lot to them because it means a lot to him," Fox said.

But the warm feelings around Bailey and the Broncos crumbled in Super Bowl XLVIII. A combination of crowd noise and miscommunication led to a safety on the first play from scrimmage, when Manny Ramirez's snap sailed past Manning and into the end zone. That wasn't the reason why the Broncos lost, but a tone had been set.

Seattle's defensive speed dismantled the Broncos' most trusted offensive weapons. The screen passes that were so perfect throughout the year were blown up by defenders closing from the back side. The offensive line was overrun from the flanks by quick pass rushers. And the Broncos' defense finally collapsed under the weight of injuries that had accumulated and by the Super Bowl had robbed them of a stellar cover cornerback (Chris Harris Jr.), a starting safety (Rahim Moore), their best pass rusher (Von Miller), their nastiest defensive tackle (Kevin Vickerson), a versatile starting defensive lineman (Derek Wolfe), and their intended starting middle linebacker (Stewart Bradley).

Every coach, including Fox, has at some point preached, "Next man up," as a mantra for overcoming injuries. Eventually, even the best teams run out of next men, and the Broncos fell, 43-8.

But the final disappointment is not to be confused with failure. Elway, Fox, and Manning had reversed the Broncos' course, ending their late 2000s descent into mediocrity. The Broncos were back among the NFL's title contenders, a spot in which they had taken residence for thirty seasons, from Red Miller to Mike Shanahan.

TRYING TO GET OVER THE HUMP

When the Broncos signed Peyton Manning in March 2012, they knew their window to win with him was limited. There was no sugar-coating multiple neck surgeries and the fact that he would turn 36 before he had his first practice as a Bronco; even if everything went right, the realistic expectation was three to four seasons.

By the end of the 2014 season, the clock was ticking loudly. Injuries had begun to accumulate for Manning, who struggled down the stretch in that season as the Broncos finished 12-4. A third consecutive season in which the Broncos earned a first-round bye ended short of a world championship, and for the second time in Manning's Broncos career, the Broncos didn't even win a playoff game.

This time, the fallout was massive. A day after a 24-13 loss to the Colts ended the 2014 season, John Fox was out as head coach by mutual decision with John Elway. Four division titles in four seasons were not enough. Fox had won everything—except what the Broncos wanted most.

Exacerbating matters was the declining health of owner Pat Bowlen. The Broncos' 43-8 loss to Super Bowl XLVIII was the last game in which Bowlen was an active part of the team. Five months later, he was forced to step away from daily ownership responsibilities because of Alzheimer's disease. The next time the Broncos made a Super Bowl, Bowlen would be unable to attend.

Elway wanted nothing more than to say, "This one's for Pat!" and complete the circle begun at San Diego's Qualcomm Stadium on Jan. 25, 1998, when the Broncos won Super Bowl XXXII over Green Bay and Bowlen handed Elway the trophy, proclaiming, "This one's for John!" Manning represented Elway's first, best chance to make this happen, but time was running out.

To make the most of Manning, Elway turned to someone he trusted more than just about anyone else in football, his old training-camp and road-trip roommate, backup quarterback and offensive coordinator Gary Kubiak.

Kubiak's presence and instincts would be crucial in pushing the Broncos to take the final step that allowed them to capitalize on Manning's presence, even as age and injuries sapped the surefire Hall of Famer's performance during an up-and-down final season.

But it would be Kubiak's defensive coordinator who would ultimately create the unit that defined the 2015 Broncos and gave them a place in NFL history.

WELCOME BACK, WADE

"What's your guess (or guesses) for DC?" one fan asked me via Twitter in January 2015 when Kubiak was looking for his boss to run the defense while he guided the offense. "Please don't say Wade Phillips."

Believe it or not, there were some vocal fans who did not want Phillips, the Broncos' head coach in 1993 and 1994 and defensive coordinator from 1989 to '92, to return as defensive coordinator when Gary Kubiak assumed the reins.

"We need to be innovative, not a 1992 reunion tour," said that tweeter.

Had he gotten his way, the Broncos wouldn't have won Super Bowl 50 because that world championship would not have been possible without Phillips arriving, changing the Broncos' alignment from a 4-3 to a 3-4 and turning loose a talented unit to do what it did best: attack.

Phillips trusted his cornerbacks to hold up their end of the bargain in man-to-man coverage, leaving Pro Bowlers Chris Harris Jr. and Aqib Talib on an island more often than not. That freed safeties and linebackers from additional coverage responsibilities, allowing them to supplement the interior pass rush provided by ends Malik Jackson and Derek Wolfe and the edge rush spearheaded by perennial Pro Bowlers Von Miller and DeMarcus Ware.

It was a perfect storm. Only nagging injuries to Ware, then a veteran of 11 seasons, held back the unit, but all that did was allow him to save his strength for a dominant playoff run in which he hit Ben Roethlisberger, Tom Brady, and Cam Newton 12 times.

What allowed Phillips to succeed and build a defense that took its place among the pantheon of the league's greats wasn't just his tactical acumen. That came naturally, of course, honed by four decades in the NFL coaching a galaxy of stars, including Hall of Famers such as Elvin Bethea, Rickey Jackson, Reggie White, and Bruce Smith—and some who should be, like Broncos legend Steve Atwater.

But Phillips kept himself culturally relevant, listening to music you wouldn't expect to find on the iPod of a coach born during the Truman administration. He even quoted Drake's "Big Rings" when asked about receiving his Super Bowl 50 hardware.

WADE'S EYES ARE EVERYWHERE

During games, they scanned the field. During the week, they studied film, probing an opposing offense for weaknesses. From time to time, they were on his phone, as he fired off one of his witty Twitter missives that included various puns or tossing shade at the Green Bay Packers after his defense dismantled them midway through the 2015 season, proclaiming, "Chicken parm tastes so good—I like it especially with cheese."

I got a firsthand look at the expanse of his gaze one day at practice in November 2015, when he took a break from watching his players warm up and walked over to the sideline where the media gathered.

"I was looking at your power rankings," he said in his south Texas drawl, "and you had us fifth!"

I had a good explanation, of course. There were a lot of numbers involved, Coach—not just the defense. The offense ranked 25th in adjusted points per possession. The team dropped in giveaway-take-away margin the last two games because of three turnovers and no takeaways forced.

Almost every week after that, Phillips would walk over to play-fully needle me about where the team ranked—even though the teams it usually trailed had better records, such as Carolina, which was on its way to a 15-1 finish that would ultimately be three games better than that of the Broncos.

Championships aren't won on spreadsheets, of course, and by the time the Broncos and Panthers met in Super Bowl 50, the Panthers' statistical advantage went out the window, buried by the manpower advantage of Von Miller and DeMarcus Ware over Panthers tackles Michael Oher and Mike Remmers.

In the confetti-strewn chaos following Super Bowl 50, Phillips spotted me and smiled.

"You got us No. 1 now?"

Yes, Wade, your team was No. 1.

The Force Awakened—With a Vengeance

Von Miller was a bit disappointed with his 2014 season, so he spent the 2015 offseason recommitting himself to a new diet. He tossed out the ice cream and fatty meats, instead opting for chicken breast and other lean meats, vegetables, fresh fruit—and water by the gallon.

But he sometimes deviated from that—especially as the 2015 season progressed. And by the time the Broncos began their playoff run toward Super Bowl 50, Miller was feeling frisky enough to eat mozzarella sticks from a movie-theater concession stand while watching *Star Wars: The Force Awakens.*

A day later, he couldn't finish practice because of gastrointestinal distress.

"You can't put just regular gas in a Ferrari," Miller said. "The force struck back."

Listen to Your Mother

When running back C.J. Anderson emerged midway through the 2014 season after a series of injuries to running backs, he galvanized the Broncos run game so much that he ended the season in the Pro Bowl in spite of not making a start until November.

With electric moves in the open field and a persistent style that allowed him to turn losses into positive yardage even when blocking broke down, Anderson's combination of darting moves and dogged determination would eventually help prove decisive in the Broncos' run to Super Bowl 50 a year later, as he plowed through a swarm of Panthers for the title-clinching touchdown.

run to Super Bowl 50 a year later, as he plowed through a swarm of Panthers for the title-clinching touchdown.

No one was prouder of Anderson that day than his mother, who along with a host of family members and friends, had made the 64-mile trip from Vallejo, California, to Santa Clara to see the Broncos' third world championship in person.

His mother pushed him while he was growing up. But his mother never stopped prodding him. Even after he made it in the NFL, she continued to critique him to the point where she was as tough on him as his position coach, Eric Studesville.

"Neck and neck," Anderson said. "Coach E, he don't let up. He just continues to keep pushing me, which I love every day. He makes sure he's on top of me. Then after that I have to deal with my biggest critic and my biggest fan when I get on the phone with her.

"She'll never pat me on the back. Never. She'll say, 'Good game,' every once in a while. She'll definitely talk about there was a lot of yards I left out there."

And she'll also critique his demeanor. Early in the 2015 season, as Anderson grappled with an ankle injury and struggled to find lanes, she had another critique.

"She called me and was like, 'You're just not having fun,'" Anderson said. "I was like, 'My mom's right.' As bad as I wanted to be wrong, she was right."

Eventually, Anderson got healthy. He found his smile. He found his form. And he found the end zone in Super Bowl 50 to give the Broncos their final push toward the promised land for the third time in franchise history.

THERE'S NO ONE LIKE PEYTON

In evaluating the impact of Peyton Manning on the Broncos, I've tried to remove recency bias from the equation. Even when doing so, I can't think of a single Broncos player who made a greater impact on the organization in such a short time.

When Manning signed with the Broncos, they'd gone five years without a winning season —their longest such streak since the club began its history with 13 consecutive .500 or worse seasons. Although the Broncos had won a playoff game the previous season with Tim Tebow at the controls, it was still a team that had yet to emerge from mediocrity.

Manning changed all that.

In his four seasons, the Broncos won fifty of the sixty-five games he started, including a 3-0 run through the 2016 postseason that allowed him to become the first quarterback since John Elway to retire as the starting quarterback of a Super Bowl champion.

It didn't matter that Manning wasn't his vintage self during that title run, that he threw nearly twice as many interceptions as touchdown passes. He still made a difference. The Broncos don't win Super Bowl 50 if Gary Kubiak doesn't call on him to relieve Brock Osweiler during the third quarter of the regular-season finale against San Diego.

With a 13-7 deficit, the offense imploding thanks to five giveaways and the home crowd nervous, Kubiak followed a "gut feeling" and put Manning in the game, even though it was the veteran's first time in uniform since he injured his foot nearly two months earlier.

When Manning strolled into the huddle, it seemed like every sports cliché about grit come to life. It was Willis Reed in the 1970 NBA Finals. It was "Daniel LaRusso's gonna fight!" in *The Karate Kid*. The stadium shook.

"It kind of seemed like he struck fear in the other defense," said Chris Harris Jr. "They were like, 'Oh, man, Peyton Manning's coming out here.'"

He guided the Broncos downfield, stabilized their hopes and led them back to a 27-20 win that kept them at home for the postseason.

An audible from Manning led directly to one touchdown pass in the AFC Championship Game, to Owen Daniels. And although his numbers were unspectacular in the postseason —his yardage went from 222 against Pittsburgh in the divisional round to just 141 in Super Bowl 50—he did just enough. He kept the Broncos on schedule. He kept the locker room on account.

And he was able to walk out a world champion.

Elway's bold free-agency gambit of March 2012 had paid off. A team that had questions at quarterback and a five-year run without a winning season had returned to the sport's summit. Manning had done his job, and on March 7, 2016, he walked away, offering as many "thank yous" as touchdown passes in his career.

"There's a Scripture reading: 2 Timothy 4:7: 'I have fought the good fight and I have finished the race; I have kept the faith,'" Manning said. "Well, I have fought the good fight, I have finished my football race, and after 18 years, it's time.

"God bless all of you, and God bless football."

And for getting four years, two AFC titles and a world championship from the game's all-time leader in passing yardage and touchdown passes, the Broncos will feel forever blessed that Manning picked them to close his brilliant career.

Fantasy Football: "It's Just Not Real"

Tens, if not hundreds, of millions of people worldwide play fantasy football. Many of them now watch the sport to see how the players on their fantasy teams do, and care little about the actual result.

Many of those same people are on social media outlets such as Twitter and Facebook. So are their players. And some of them are all too quick to register their disappointment— quite often with hostile words unsuitable for a book geared toward family audiences.

Early in the 2015 season, no one absorbed more punishment than C.J. Anderson. Expected to be the bell-cow running back in a Gary Kubiak-led offense that would be more run-centric, Anderson was slowed by ankle injuries and ended up splitting time with Ronnie Hillman, who proved to be more productive early in the season because of better health. Anderson gamely soldiered on through the pain, never revealing the severity of the ankle injury.

The fantasy players who used high-round draft picks on Anderson cared not one bit about his ankle, or about injuries and instability on the offensive line in the wake of Ryan Clady's season-ending torn anterior cruciate ligament. They just saw no touchdowns in his first six games of the 2015 season, and they wanted blood. With the digital-media equivalent of pitchforks and torches, they came after Anderson, lambasting him for his lack of touchdowns.

Anderson didn't care.

"Everybody wants to talk about it and throw you in there, give you so many points. It's just not real," Anderson said. "What's real is what we do every day on that football field. I just try to go out there and help my team win."

"I tell people, 'You can sit me for 17 weeks, and I don't care.' I saw something on ESPN [asking], 'Was C.J. Anderson a fantasy bust?'

I wish I could call ESPN and say, 'Tell them to drop me. Every owner can drop me. I don't care at all.'"

FAREWELL, KUBIAK

The March 2016 goodbye to Peyton Manning was entirely expected.

The Jan. 2, 2017 retirement of Gary Kubiak was anything but.

After winning Super Bowl 50 in his first season back with the team, it seemed like Kubiak was poised for a long run on the team's sideline. The transition out of the Manning era would surely provide some bumps, and the 9-7 finish in 2016 with Trevor Siemian and Paxton Lynch at quarterback reflected the inconsistent nature of the campaign and the offensive struggles in particular. But Kubiak was set to be the steady hand to navigate the Broncos through the choppy waters.

All that changed in Week 5, when the Broncos lost to the Atlanta Falcons and Kubiak left the home stadium in the back of an ambulance. A complex migraine condition was the diagnosis, and he sat out the trip to San Diego four days later, leaving special teams coordinator Joe DeCamillis in charge for the 21-13 defeat.

It was the second time in four seasons in which Kubiak needed an ambulance to leave the stadium. In Houston three years earlier, he suffered a transient-ischemic attack—colloquially called a "mini-stroke"—as he walked off the field at halftime that sidelined him for a week. It was the combination of the two incidents, and his understanding of his own tendencies as a head coach, that led him to decide to walk away.

Kubiak knew himself well. He knew he couldn't surrender the offensive play-calling duties he loved so much. If he could have removed his hands from the offensive reins, he might have extended his coaching career. But he couldn't bring himself to do it, and after a season in which he "struggled big-time," he walked away.

"I've looked at a lot of things, how to do this different and that different, but the bottom line is that's the way I'm wired," he said. "And when I do something, that's the way I'm going to go about it."

One day after he coached his final game, he stepped up to the lectern of the team meeting room at Broncos headquarters carrying a battered leather folio he'd had with him for 25 seasons. He got it during his first season as a coach, when he guided running backs at Texas A&M in 1992. It stayed with him at every stop: from the San Francisco 49ers to 11 seasons as the Broncos' offensive coordinator to eight seasons as Houston Texans head coach to a campaign as Baltimore's offensive coordinator before going back to Denver in 2015.

He thought that the folio would outlast his coaching career.

"I used to joke with some of these coaches that when this book falls apart, I'm done. I'm out," he said as he made his farewell remarks.

"Well, it tore this morning."

And a few minutes later, Kubiak was out the door, taking with him the memories carved during 22 seasons as a player, assistant coach, and a head coach with the Broncos. Six of those seasons ended in Super Bowl appearances. Three saw world championships. Just two of them witnessed losing records.

Kubiak wasn't always at the forefront of the Broncos. But he was always a winner, and will always be a legendary part of the organization.

ACKNOWLEDGMENTS

This book would not have been possible without the wealth of gamebooks and post-game press conference transcripts offered by the Broncos in the online archive created by their public-relations department. To the staffers past and present, particularly Mark Cicero, Paul Kirk, Erich Schubert, Patrick Smyth, Rebecca Villanueva, my deepest thanks for a database that allowed me to fill in the blanks of my own memory. A special thanks is owed to Jim Saccomano, the Broncos' long-time communications guru (with various titles over the decades), and to Niels Aaboe and Skyhorse Publishing for their patience. Thanks to all the players and coaches who have answered my questions and those of others on the Broncos beat over the last twelve years. And finally, to my wife, Amy, who has accepted my odd hours and peculiar work habits, and my dogs, Rupert and George, who kept me company as I typed in my home office.

"I started it with them, their doin' it," said running back Edgerrin James.

"I think that was the key moment," offered tight end Marcus Pollard, who watched with James from the sideline. "Everybody kind of decided, 'This thing is for real. Let's slide it in and put one on them.' That set the tone for the rest of the game."

It won't happen again. The NFL cut in on the dance.

The league deemed it "taunting" and announced during the March 2004 owners meeting that any further instance would result in a 15-yard penalty. Mike Pereira, the league's director of officiating, said unsportsmanlike conduct and taunting could be points of emphasis in 2004, and the Colts' jig is a big suggestion.

"I think it's taunting," he said. "Its 31 guys doing a choreographed thing.

"Because they were doing it when it was tied, on the opening kickoff.

"Then we're going to have to consider it," Pereira said. "It's a group demonstration and that's not going to be allowed."

And that's that.

"It was fun while it lasted," said owner Jim Irsay.

Simpler Can Be Better

The Cover 2 defense that Tony Dungy brought to the Colts and defensive coordinator Ron Meeks oversaw was many things, simple chief among them.

Safety Idrees Bashir estimated that the Colts ran an "over 33 coverages in 2001, when Vic Fangio coordinated the defense and Jim Mora was head coach. That number, Bashir

BIBLIOGRAPHY

Anderson, Dave, "Miller and Surprising Broncos: From Bust to Best," *New York Times* News Service, December 3, 1977.

Associated Press, "11-5 Broncos are home for the holidays," *Beaver County Times*, December 23, 1985.

Associated Press, "Baltimore files a grievance against Denver," *The Tuscaloosa News*, August 11, 1983.

Associated Press, "Bitter but better is Lend-Lease Lee" *The Spokesman-Review*, August 4, 1966.

Associated Press, "Broncos buck Big Red," *The Southeast Missourian*, September 19, 1977.

Associated Press, "Broncos 'crush' Steelers' hopes," *Sarasota Herald-Tribune*, December 25, 1977.

Associated Press, "Broncos decide on Weese," *The Spokesman-Review*, August 28, 1979.

Associated Press, "Broncos, Elway happy, but not everyone else," *Sarasota Herald-Tribune*, May 4, 1983.

Associated Press, "Broncos head to Buffalo without Elway," *Moscow-Pullman Daily News*, December 11, 1992.

Associated Press, "Broncos refuse solidarity shake," *The Southeast Missourian*, August 15, 1982.

Associated Press, "Broncos tap body-builder Poole," *Pittsburgh Post-Gazette*, October 12, 1987.

Associated Press, "Bucs return to site of McKay's memorable tirade," *Ocala Star-Banner*, December 24, 1983.

Associated Press, "Craig Morton steps down," *Daytona Beach Morning Journal*, November 25, 1982.

Associated Press, "Elway booed to bench, but DeBerg beats Colts," *The Sumter Daily Item*, September 12, 1983.

Associated Press, "Elway lifts Denver into playoffs," *The Lewiston Daily Sun*, December 13, 1983.

Associated Press, "Fairy tale Super Bowl?" *The Nevada Daily Mail*, December 23, 1977.

Associated Press, "Fierce Oiler defence rocks Broncos," *The Montreal Gazette*, December 24, 1979.

Associated Press, "For Broncos, playing is the easy part," *Reading Eagle*, October 27, 1997.

Associated Press, "Little's home finale emotional—4-star," *Reading Eagle*, December 15, 1975.

Associated Press, "No changes coming for playoff system," *The Tuscaloosa News*, December 24, 1985.

Associated Press, "Patriots thought they would come back," *The Lakeland Ledger*, January 4, 1987.

Associated Press, "Reeves impressed by Browns' offense," *The Schnectady Gazette*, Janauary 19, 1988.

Associated Press, "This season, Mecklenburg has settled in," *Reading Eagle*, January 27, 1988.

Associated Press, "Upset! Broncos ride herd on Raiders, 30-7," *Daytona Beach Morning Journal*, October 17, 1977.

Barreiro, Dan, "Ex-mates Morton, Reeves reunited to lead Broncos," *The Dallas Morning News*, October 15, 1981.

Bouchette, Ed, "Broncos storm back to contention after miserable 1990," *Pittsburgh Post-Gazette*, November 1, 1991.

Brady, Dave, "Rozelle to question Broncos about injury to Morton," *The Milwaukee Journal* via the *Washington Post* Service, January 3, 1978.

Brooks, Janet, "Canadian fulfills football dream in Denver," *The Montreal Gazette*, November 24, 1984.

Chapin, Dwight, "The Toughest 49 Ever," *The Coffin Corner:* Vol. 15, No. 6, 1993.

Chick, Bob, "Haven Moses," *The Evening Independent*, January 11, 1978.

"Broncos President and CEO Pat Bowlen answers your questions," *DenverBroncos.com*, March 11, 2005.

"Offensive coordinator Gary Kubiak gives his answers," *DenverBroncos.com*, April 8, 2005.

"Spanning the Decades: Floyd Little Q&A," *DenverBroncos.com*, June 23, 2006.

"Spanning the Decades: Lionel Taylor Q&A," *DenverBroncos.com*, June 16, 2006.

"Super Bowl XXXII Memories, Brian Habib," *DenverBroncos.com*, January 22, 2008.

"Super Bowl XXXII Memories, Glenn Cadrez," *DenverBroncos.com*, January 25, 2008.

"Super Bowl XXXII Memories, John Elway," *DenverBroncos.com*, February 3, 2008.

"Super Bowl XXXII Memories, John Mobley," *DenverBroncos.com*, January 29, 2008.

"Super Bowl XXXII Memories, Shannon Sharpe," *DenverBroncos.com*, January 11, 2008.

"Super Bowl XXXII Memories, Steve Atwater," *DenverBroncos.com*, January 18, 2008.

Dolch, Craig, "Denver comeback beats Cleveland 23-20 in™," *The Palm Beach Post*, January 12, 1987.

Gentilviso, Chris, "A Toast to Two Football Visionaries," *DenverBroncos.com*, November 8, 2009.

Gola, Hank, "Broncos and Patriots have come long way since playing in first AFL game 53 years ago," *New York Daily News*, January 18, 2014.

Hoffer, Richard, "Happy Days," *Sports Illustrated*, August 2, 1993.

Jenkins, Dan, "Wholly Moses for Denver," *Sports Illustrated*, January 9, 1978.

Marshall, Brian, "The Pro Football Career of Cookie Gilchrist," *The Coffin Corner*: Vol. 24, No. 2, 2000.

Merilatt, James, "Gary Zimmerman earns his rightful spot in the Ring of Fame," *DenverBroncos.com*, September 27, 2003.

Mizell, Hubert. "McKay: Ralston's day is coming," *St. Petersburg Times*, November 9, 1976.

Molinari, Dave, "The Broncos $5 million man begins earning his pay today," *The Pittsburgh Press*, September 4, 1983.

Moss, Irv, "Colorado Classics: Former Broncos offensive lineman Dave Studdard," *The Denver Post*, August 21, 2012.

Moss, Irv, "Howsam 'believed in Denver,'" *The Denver Post*, February 20, 2008.

O'Brien, Jim, "Even in fatal battle, McCabe a winner," *The Pittsburgh Press*, January 3, 1983.

Reilly, Rick, "Driven," *Sports Illustrated*, January 13, 1992.

Saccomano, Jim, *Denver Broncos: The Complete Illustrated History*, Minneapolis: MBI Publishing Company, 2009.

Saunders, Patrick, "Turn out the lights ...," *The Denver Post*, November 13, 2000.

Shrake, Edwin, "Denver Broncos," *Sports Illustrated*, September 13, 1965.

Sonneman, Kyle, "Spanning the Decades: Frank Tripucka," *DenverBroncos.com*, June 14, 2006.

Stellino, Vito. "All Broncos want is respect," *Pittsburgh Post-Gazette*, November 4, 1977.

Strother, Shelby. "Cookie Gilchrist will tell all … for a price," *The Denver Post* via *The Tuscaloosa News*, August 10, 1983.

Sports Illustrated staff, "Strong Get Stronger," *Sports Illustrated*, September 18, 1967.

Underwood, John, "Mile-High Hopes in High Old Denver," *Sports Illustrated*, October 22, 1962.

United Press International, "Denver Broncos upset Patriots," *Reading Eagle*, September 10, 1960.

United Press International, "Denver offence suspect—Coach Miller," *The Montreal Gazette*, December 24, 1979.

United Press International, "Grid Giants trade Morton to Broncos," *The Schenectady Gazette*, March 8, 1977.

United Press International, "Like Fran Tarkenton last year, Craig Morton plays down injury," *Boca Raton News*, January 11, 1978.

United Press International, "Morton has given Broncos more than they bargained for," *Boca Raton News*, January 5, 1978.

United Press International, "Morton leads stunning comeback," *Ellensburg Daily Record*, September 24, 1979.

United Press International, "Ralston will stay—despite the pressure," *The Deseret News*, December 25, 1976.

United Press International, "Reeves is coach, Alderman general manager of Broncos," *Lodi News-Sentinel*, March 11, 1981.

United Press International, "Struggling Broncos bench Elway," *The Montreal Gazette*, October 6, 1983.

Vecsey, George, "Sports of the Times: Karlis, Barefoot Soldier," *The New York Times*, January 23, 1987.

Vischansky, Peter, "The Life and Times of Fred Gehrke," *The Coffin Corner:* Vol. 22, No. 3, 2000.

Wiley, Ralph, "Getting better and better," *Sports Illustrated*, November 10, 1986.

Wire service reports, "Broncos sign English basketball player," *Spokane Chronicle*, April 27, 1990.

Wire service reports, "Coley asks: What's all the fuss?" *St. Petersburg Times*, November 9, 1976.

Wire service reports, "Former coach of Broncos still wondering why," *Eugene-Register Guard*, January 18, 1987.

Wojciechowski, Gene, "Once a coach, Red Miller is … wheeling and dealing," *Los Angeles Times*, January 31, 1988.

Wojciechowski, Gene, "Shula, Noll overlooked as coaches?" *Dallas Morning News*, January 5, 1985.

Zimmer, Larry. *Denver Broncos: Colorful Tales of the Orange and Blue*, Guilford, Connecticut: The Globe Pequot Press, 2004.

Zimmerman, Paul. "Denver Is Standing Mile High Once Again," *Sports Illustrated*, October 19, 1981.

Zimmerman, Paul. "There Was No Bucking These Broncos," *Sports Illustrated*, October 8, 1984.